372.3
Tch   Tchudi, Stephen, 1942-
       Probing the unknown :
       from myth to science

DATE DUE			
5			
0 2			

372.3
Tch   Tchudi, Stephen, 1942-
       Probing the unknown :
       from myth to science

GAYLORD M2

PROBING THE
UNKNOWN

PROBING THE
UNKNOWN

FROM MYTH TO SCIENCE

STEPHEN TCHUDI

CHARLES SCRIBNER'S SONS · NEW YORK

Charles Scribner's Sons Books for Young Readers
Macmillan Publishing Company, 866 Third Avenue · New York, NY 10022
Collier Macmillan Canada, Inc.

Printed in the United States of America
First Edition   10 9 8 7 6 5 4 3 2 1

Illustrations on pages 2, 50, 61, 63, 78, 87, 96, and 98 by Jackie Aher.

Library of Congress Cataloging-in-Publication Data
Tchudi, Stephen.
Probing the unknown: from myth to science / Stephen Tchudi.
—1st ed. p. cm.   Includes bibliographical references.
1. Science—Study and teaching (Elementary)
2. Astronomy—Study and teaching (Elementary) 3. Myth. I. Title.
LB1585.T39 1990   372.3'5044—dc20
89–35938 CIP AC   ISBN 0-684-19086-9

For Noodle Users Everywhere

Contents

Foreword

The idea for this book came on a cool, rainy day in London, England. I was riding one of those red double-decker buses when I met the fare collector who inspired me. This man's job involved walking from one end of the bus to the other, upstairs and downstairs. He calculated fares, collected money, and cranked out tickets from a small machine that hung at his waist. After he gave me my receipt, he said, "Look at it rain out there. It's been an awful summer here. Too much rain. Too cold. I think it's that comet that's coming, the one that comes every seventy-six years."

The comet was the one named Halley's, and it was visible that summer whenever the rain clouds weren't too thick.

The conductor added, "I think I'll light my cigarette off that comet's tail as it goes by!"

He went on, "They say nobody knows how large the universe is. Well, if they'd use the old noodle it seems to me they could figure it out from that comet. They know how fast it's going or they wouldn't know when to expect it. From that they could figure how far it travels in seventy-six years; so if you divided by two, that would tell you how far it is to the edge of the universe."

Probing the unknown.

That's what my fare collector was doing. He was using the old noo-dle to figure out the answer to a pretty interesting question: How far it is to the edge of outer space?

As it turns out, his idea was wrong.

He assumed that Halley's comet actually travels to the *edge* of the universe and then returns. Astronomers tell us that's not the case. Halley's goes only a fraction of the way out into the great darkness of space before the sun's gravity pulls it back.

He also was wrong in thinking the comet was hot, that he could light a cigarette from its tail. Scientists have determined that Halley's comet is actually made up of ice. What looks like a fiery tail is a stream of small ice particles, stretching out in a trail, reflecting sun-light, and thus appearing to glow.

My fare collector was also probably wrong in assuming that a comet, millions of miles away in outer space, was causing it to be cold and rainy in London. Nevertheless, I was impressed by the way he was using his mind to try to understand one of the mysteries of the universe—*How far is it to the edge?*—and that's how he inspired this book. (I even saved the fare receipt that he gave me.)

Probing the Unknown describes some of the ways in which human beings raise questions and come up with answers about mysteries in the world.

An Aztec Indian poem expresses an interesting philosophy:

> Who am I?
> As a bird I fly about
> Seeing things, partaking of things.
> Let my heart be delighted with them.

Ours is a fascinating and puzzling universe, something that can cause us great delight as we study it. I hope this book will help you come to appreciate probing the unknown for yourself.

To help you apply the ideas in this book, I will occasionally suggest ideas to explore. These sections, which will be boxed, are intended to get you:

PROBING ON YOUR OWN

On a sheet of paper (or using index cards), list some of the questions you have about the world in which you live. Some questions may have to do with comets, or stars, or the planets. Others may center on small worlds like those of insects or microbes. You may be puzzled about people questions: Why do people behave the way they do? Why is there meanness? What makes people happy? You might write down questions about topics covered in school (reading, art, music, geography) or about hobbies you pursue outside of school (reading, art, music, skateboards). You can list questions about how things work, why things don't work. You can wonder about the future or the past. No question is a silly one. Save your list. Perhaps use it as a bookmark. Add questions as you read along. This book will not even attempt to answer all questions or even most questions, but from time to time you can think about ways in which you could find answers. That's what *Probing the Unknown* is all about.

1

Legends and Myths

In the state of Michigan, lying along the shore of Lake Michigan, is a national park called the Sleeping Bear Dunes. The park includes some huge sand dunes—over four hundred feet high—which rise up out of the lake like cliffs.

The dunes are mostly sand, but in places they are covered by vegetation, sometimes small bushes, sometimes pine trees, whose roots have found a grip in the sandy soil. If you look at the dunes from a distance, you can sometimes make out what seem to be shapes in the pattern of green vegetation on sand. Just as you can study clouds and imagine figures—whales, dinosaurs, faces—some people say that at Sleeping Bear they can see the outline of what looks like a giant black bear dozing on the sand.

The Legend of Sleeping Bear

In her book about the legend of Sleeping Bear, Gloria Sproul writes: "Somewhere, in some part of Michigan, close to the site of Sleeping Bear, a creative Indian mother, father, Chief, or child spun the tale, which was to live on in the hearts and minds of generations of people for hundreds of years."

Sleeping Bear Dunes

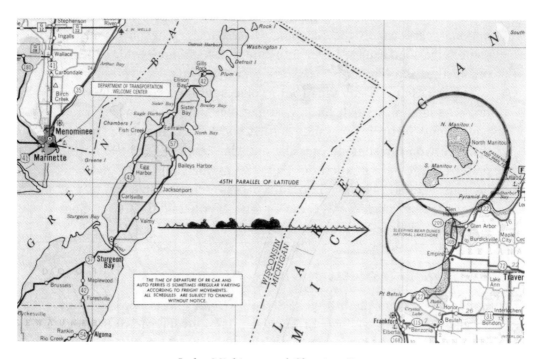

Lake Michigan and Sleeping Bear
Reprinted by permission of the Michigan Department of Transportation.

The story is part of the lore of the Algonquin Indians, and it has been told and retold in many different forms. The basic story goes like this:

> Once, long ago, a great mother bear lived with her two cubs in the land that has since become Wisconsin, on the western shore of Lake Michigan. One dry summer day, lightning started a monstrous forest fire, destroying trees, killing many animals. The mother bear knew of only one way to protect her cubs, and that was to herd them into the waters of the great lake. She knew about a safe, wooded land to the east, across the lake, so, with cubs following, she swam toward Michigan. The cubs were good swimmers, but they were not as strong as the mother, and first one, then the other slipped beneath the water. When the mother reached the Michigan shore, she hauled herself onto the dunes and lay waiting for her babies. They never appeared, and so she continued her watching, day and night, year in and year out. The great spirit, Manitou, eventually took pity. He recovered the two drowned cubs from the depths of the lake and created two offshore islands, which he named the Manitou Islands after himself.

You can see the setting for this story on the map. To the left is Wisconsin, to the east, Michigan. You can see the route the bears would have taken in swimming the seventy miles across Lake Michigan. You may or may not think that North and South Manitou islands look much like the forms of bear cubs, but that doesn't really change the power of the story.

Defining "Myth" and "Legend"

We know that the patch of trees on the dunes is *not* a sleeping bear, nor are the Manitou Islands a pair of cubs. The Indians who created the legend certainly knew that as well.

One common definition of a myth or a legend is "a story that isn't true." A legend is a story that has been passed down from one generation to another. Often it's a story that started out "true" but changed over time, probably growing more fantastic along the way. A myth is also a story passed down through the ages. The main difference is that myths are usually about superheroes and heroines, gods and goddesses, powerful animals and monsters, while legends present tales about ordinary people and animals. To dismiss myths and legends as *false* would be to miss the point; both of them deal with a kind of "truth." Myths and legends help us understand the unknown.

Both legends and myths are part of an oral storytelling tradition. Both were passed on by word of mouth for years and years, which explains how they became exaggerated and why you can often find several versions of a myth or legend.

Just about every group of people who live together have their own collection of stories. There are national myths and legends that find their way into the books, but many local and regional tales are never written down and remain part of oral folklore. Many of these tales have been around for centuries or even for thousands of years. As I will show you at the close of this chapter, we're even creating myths and legends today.

In the United States, we have a wonderful collection of myths and legends from some of the original settlers of this country—not the Pilgrims and the European settlers (although they, too, had their own stories to tell), but the original inhabitants of the land, the American Indians, who were here long before 1492. Their stories are filled with powerful gods and legendary people as well as some ordinary people who do unusual and fantastic things.

An Indian Creation Myth

Almost every culture has a set of creation myths, stories about how the world is imagined to have begun. The Algonquin Indians explain that the world was created by the Sky Chief, Gitchi Manitou, the same god who raised the bear cubs from the lake and gave his name to the islands they became. The Sky Chief lived somewhere in the heavens, and below him, beneath the clouds, was the earth, completely covered by water. Gitchi Manitou had a daughter, Ataensic (pronounced Ah-tah-en-sick), who became ill and, to everyone's great sorrow, died.

"But wait a minute," you may be saying. "If this is a story about how things *began,* how is it that a god and his daughter already existed, along with heaven and earth?"

That's a good question and one that this myth doesn't answer. As you examine myths from different cultures, you will see that they do not always explain *everything* in a strictly logical fashion. You can imagine an impatient storyteller, perhaps a village elder, replying to such a question:

"Never mind where the Sky Chief and the heavens and earth came from. That's not the point of the story."

The point of this story is that Ataensic was buried under the roots of a great oak tree, along with the skins of animals: the fox, the seal, the beaver, the otter, the muskrat, the duck, small turtles, and even a frog.

"A great tree? Foxes? Seals? You mean they were already created, too?"

"Yes, in the heavens. But these were not earthly creatures nor an earthly oak tree. These were a part of the heavens, the magical world of the gods."

There followed a great earthquake, and Ataensic and the skins buried with her were shaken loose and fell from the sky, heading toward earth, which was, as I said, all water, no land. It was called the "endless sea."

Ataensic's fall was broken by some birds who gently caught her. "Birds?" you ask.

"Yes. Birds had already been created by the Gitchi Manitou."

Just as the birds were about to set her down on the water, a great turtle rose up from the sea, and Ataensic and the skins—which had now been transformed back into live animals—landed on the back of the turtle.

Details about what hapened next vary from one version of the story to another. Some storytellers said that chunks of soil from the great oak in the heavens fell with Ataensic, who used them to coat the back of the turtle, thus creating dry land. Others say that the animals took turns diving deep into the sea, looking for something solid. Most of them failed, but the frogs succeeded in bringing up bits of muck from the ocean bottom, and this was plastered over the back of the turtle. Whatever the details, the stories have in common that the earth as we know it was created in this way—soil covering the back of the giant turtle to construct the land mass.

Interestingly, quite close to Sleeping Bear Dunes, at the very top of Michigan's lower peninsula, is Mackinac Island (pronounced "Mackinaw"). It is also called Turtle Island because of its shape (see the map). Now, it takes some imagination to see the shape of a turtle in the outline of this island, but the purpose of the myth is to explain some part of the unknown, not necessarily to present a clear and "scientific" truth. If the great turtle were a part of your myths and legends, and if you'd heard about the story from childhood, you, too, would be able to "see" a turtle in the outline of an island. Remember, too, that the Indians did not have an overhead view of the island; their sketches were done from walking or canoeing around it, and without precise mapmaking tools.

Myths do not end with the creation of the earth, of course. Indian folklore is filled with fascinating stories that explain how things and people came into being. One myth explains that Ataensic gave birth to twins, and these two became Light and Darkness. The twin of light helped to create mountains, valleys, forests, deer, fruit, and, of course, daytime. The other twin created night, hurricanes and other storms, and reptiles.

Still, these twins were gods, not flesh-and-blood people. Human beings came about when the gods were told to bury the skins of animals, each with a drop of a god's blood. After four days, human

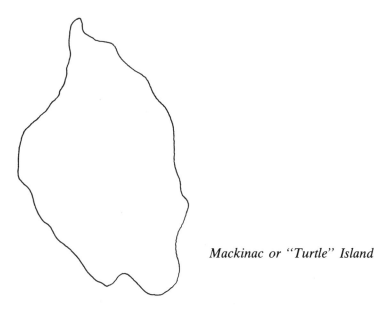

Mackinac or "Turtle" Island

beings were born from the earth and each took on some of the traits of the animal from whose skin he or she was created. Thus if you were born from a fox skin, you were crafty. People grown from a moose hide had reddish skin and were brave and powerful; those grown from rabbit skins were white and cowardly. Born of a mountain lion skin? You were a leaper. Fashioned from a musk ox? You would be clumsy and slow.

Of course, the Indians based their stories upon the world about them. Their myths tell of beaver, moose, and the wolverine. Every culture creates myths to explain what it knows. If we jump to another part of the world, we can expect to find different myths and legends to explain different circumstances.

Hawaiian Mythology

The myths of the Hawaiians, the native South Sea people who lived in the islands before the arrival of white men, explain in a different way how their world came about—a tropical world of volcano-created islands where life centers around the ocean. Judith Graham explains that in a long mythological poem, the *Kumulipo,* the Hawaiians described the world as growing out of "slime" and darkness

> At a time when the earth became hot
> At the time when the heavens turned about
> At the time when the sun was darkened
> To cause the moon to shine . . .
> The slime, this was the source of the earth
> The source of the darkness that made darkness
> The source of the night that made night
> The intense darkness, the deep darkness
> Darkness of the sun, darkness of the night
> Nothing but night.

This sounds like a dangerous and frightening time, but there were no human beings on earth to experience danger and fear. Over a long period of time, the darkness began giving birth to many creatures. These were not the beavers and wolverines of North America, of course. Hawaiian mythology tells of corals, starfish, sea cucumbers, and sea urchins. The darkness also created rough seas and storms, along with the volcanoes that, in turn, produced the islands.

You can see some interesting "scientific" truths in myths. The Hawaiian islands actually did rise out of the sea as underwater volcanoes piled up lava over millions of years. The American Indian creation myth that we looked at earlier also hints at a fact of geology: Some of our continents were actually created by great plates of earth rising up from the sea, rather like the hard shell of a turtle.

In the Hawaiian tales, people seem to have been created right along with the fish and animals, all emerging from that darkness:

> The night is swollen with plump creatures . . .
> The night gives birth to clinging creatures.

As more and more creatures were born, the night shrank, thus allowing for daytime. There, too, you can see a connection with the Indian myth. Most creation myths include an explanation of how day and night came into being.

The *Kumulipo* is also interesting because some of its verses offer explanations of thoughts and dreams. Children sprang forth from the brain of one of the Hawaiian goddesses, and these were Thoughtfulness and Dreaming.

Thus myths and legends do more than explain the mysteries of the clouds, the seas, the sky and stars. They often try to explain one of the deepest mysteries of all: What makes people tick? Why do people behave the way they do? Many myths and legends actually teach people the difference between good and evil.

The Trickster

One fascinating character who appears in mythologies all around the world is called the Trickster. In Hawaiian mythology, his name is *Maui.* In Scandinavia, he is *Loki.* The Algonquin Indians have a trickster, too, and his name is Manitou (but not *Gitchi* Manitou, the Sky Chief and great father). Sometimes, the trickster shows up as an animal: as a rabbit, a snake, a raven, or even a spider.

The trickster is basically a "bad boy," somebody who doesn't know the difference between right and wrong. He is forever trying to trick other people to get things he wants. Along the way, however, he is sometimes tricked himself, and he often winds up as a loser, which helps show that you just can't get away with trickery and deceit.

In the American Southwest, there are a number of stories about a trickster named Coyote. For example, it seems that one day Coyote was very hungry, and he spotted Turkey in a tree. Knowing that he couldn't climb up the tree, Coyote decided to trick his feathered lunch into coming down.

"I could climb up there and eat you," Coyote lied, "but you could save me the trouble by coming down here."

Turkey was not too smart, but he knew better than to leave his perch. "No, I'll just stay right here."

"Well," said Coyote, "I guess I'll have to come up and get you. Now hold still, and whatever you do, don't fly out to the prairie, because I could never catch you there!"

Hearing Coyote's words, Turkey said to himself:

"So Coyote can't catch me on the prairie! I'll just fly down there and escape!"

Turkeys are not very good at flying, so when Turkey tried to fly, he made it only a few feet before he fell to the earth, and Coyote gobbled him up.

The End.

You might find that story familiar. It is the first cousin of another tale, in which the tricky and carefree Brother Rabbit, having been stuck to the Tar Baby (fooled by another trickster, Brother Fox), manages to get himself tossed into the safety of the briar patch by claiming that's exactly where he doesn't want to be.

As you read the Coyote story, you might have recognized a TV cartoon character: Wile E. (pronounced like *wily*) Coyote, a modern-day trickster who spends his days trying to capture, blow up, or smash the Roadrunner. Even though Wile E. Coyote cartoons are amusing, one has to recognize that the Coyote is a pretty bad character: His aim is to destroy the Roadrunner, who is saved only by outwitting his enemy.

Yet another cartoon trickster, perhaps the most famous of them all, is Bugs Bunny. Now, Bugs is a rather likable rabbit, but if you think about it, you realize that he will play just about any kind of trick to get what he wants. Sometimes he acts in a good cause, to help other animals or simply to save his own skin, but often Bugs is pretty mean, playing tricks, stealing carrots, making life miserable for Elmer Fudd. Sometimes, too, Bugs gets his comeuppance—typical of the Trickster—by pigging out on stolen carrots, say, and giving himself a stomachache.

One value of these stories is that they also serve to *teach*. They say: Don't trust strangers; think carefully before you act; don't stray too far from the safety of home. Many myths and legends serve this function one way or another; they are collections of advice on how to behave in unfamiliar situations.

PROBING ON YOUR OWN

Make a study of Trickster characters on Saturday-morning TV cartoons. You'll find many of them, not only in the animal cartoons (Bugs, Daffy, Sylvester) but among the human beings portrayed there (Yosemite Sam, Reginald van Buren). As you study these tricksters, consider how modern cartoon "myths" are a part of a very old tradition of Trickster stories.

Greek and Roman Myths

It may seem like a big jump from the creation myths, which involve powerful gods and goddesses as well as storms, thunder, darkness, and great seas, to the antics of happy rogues like Bugs Bunny.

For a long time, scholars thought that myths were simply "incorrect" explanations of the world by people who didn't have very accurate science, who were victims of tall tales and superstitions. Thus if a people didn't know enough science to understand the origins of the universe, they made up stories about great turtles or life-giving darkness.

However, the more closely we examine myths, the more fully we realize that they do much more. Let's face it, life itself can sometimes be mysterious and frightening. From the beginning of recorded history, people have worried about good and evil, dying, growing up, growing old, and just plain surviving, sometimes in a world that is quite dangerous.

Nowhere is the full power of myths and legends more evident than in the stories of the Greeks and the Romans. These have been passed down to us by poets, storytellers, and playwrights who lived two to three thousand years ago. You probably have studied or will study

Greek and Roman mythology in school, since it forms important background for our culture. You'll find many references to Greek and Roman mythological characters in literature and even in the daily newspaper. We have named planets, constellations, cities, towns, streets, and even spacecraft after these gods and goddesses, and their names have been woven into hundreds of words in our language.

The Greeks created most of these mythical characters; later the Romans adopted them. Thus you'll often see two names for the gods and goddesses. Zeus, the king of the gods in Greek mythology, becomes Jupiter in Roman myths. His wife was Hera in Greece and Juno in Rome. See the chart of the gods and goddesses to compare the Greek and Roman names, to understand what they represented, and to examine some of the ways they have become part of our life and language.

Like Hawaiian and American Indian mythology, Greco-Roman mythology also begins with a creation story. The Greeks imagined the earth emerging from something called Chaos, which was a void or great nothingness, perhaps like the vacuum of outer space. From Chaos came Night and Day and a world that was mostly water. (Again you can see some similarities to the American Indian and Hawaiian stories.) The Greeks said the world was a flat disk surrounded by River Ocean, which they described as a serpent with its tail in its mouth. Day and Night gave birth to a race of Titans, or giants, and from these were born the gods, including Zeus/Jupiter, the king of the gods.

At first the earth was peaceful enough; it celebrated ages of gold, silver, and bronze, metals that represent wealth and prosperity. But the gods got into a power struggle during an age of iron in which they forged weapons. The gods fought with and defeated the Titans, establishing Zeus/Jupiter on his throne. Zeus was said to live on Mount Olympus, which is a real mountain in Greece.

During these immense struggles, human beings were created. The god Prometheus and his brother, Epimetheus, had been assigned the job of putting living creatures on earth. Epimetheus was responsible

Some Greek and Roman Gods and Goddesses

Greek	*Roman*	*Characteristics*
Zeus	Jupiter	Thunder king; king of the gods. His name has been given to the largest planet in our solar system. "By Jupiter" or "By Zeus" are often used as mild curses, but mostly in comic books.
Hera	Juno	Queen of the gods. "Junoesque" is a word often applied to a striking or "god-like" woman.
Ares	Mars	The god of war. The planet Mars is named after him because of its red color—blood-red, a battle color. "Martial" music is the music of war.
Haephestus	Vulcan	Blacksmith to the gods; said to cause volcanoes on earth as his giant forge spits out fire. "Vulcanized" rubber has been heat treated to make it stretchy.
Athena	Minerva	Goddess of wisdom. The Greeks named their cultural center, Athens, after her.
Hermes	Mercury	Winged messenger of the gods. A "Mercury" car is so named because of its swiftness. A "mercurial" person changes characters and moods swiftly.
Aphrodite	Venus	Goddess of love and beauty. An "aphrodisiac" is a love potion. A Venus's-flytrap tempts an insect into its jaws by its attractiveness. "Venusian" can be a person from one of the most beautiful planets in the solar system. A "Venus in blue jeans" is an attractive girl.
Eros	Cupid	A god of love. "Erotic" has to do with love. "Cupid" is well known as a symbol of St. Valentine's Day.

for passing out traits to the animals: strength, speed, cunning, courage, claws, wings. When it came time to create humankind, no traits worth much were left, so human beings turned out weaker and slower than most of the other animals.

Prometheus helped us out, however, and gave humankind two gifts: the ability to walk upright (so we can look at the stars rather than at the ground) and fire (which allowed us to create civilization).

Prometheus angered the gods by giving these gifts to humans, and among other punishments, he was chained to a rock, where a giant

Jupiter, overlooking the world

Minerva, goddess of wisdom

Neptune, king of the sea

Mercury, the gods' messenger

eagle ate away his innards. The character of Prometheus gives people the sense that at least one of the gods is on their side. Even in his pain, Prometheus was also a kind of trickster. He fooled the great god Zeus into eating animal guts, thinking they were good food.

Zeus had tricks of his own. He sent a beautiful and charming woman, Pandora, to earth. She could sing and dance and was described as a "gift of the gods" to humankind. Prometheus, in chains, warned the humans to be cautious about any gift from Zeus, but they accepted Pandora joyfully.

Zeus had given Pandora a small box, and he ordered her not to open it. Pandora disregarded the command and opened the box. Out flew human miseries: plague, illness and suffering, envy, spite, revenge. These escaped into the world. Pandora slammed the lid down, but only one thing remained in the box, something good: hope. Thus human beings have the power to put up with evil and bad fortune—they always possess hope.

PROBING ON YOUR OWN

In our time, people have argued that the Greeks and Romans presented a stereotyped or one-sided view of the relationships between men and women. For the most part the men were lusty, robust warriors, true macho types, while the women were portrayed as either pretty-but-dumb or scheming and witchy. In our time, a mythology about men and women would be quite different. What would a modern "king of the gods" be like? What would he value? What would the "queen of the gods" do? How might the story of Pandora be different if it were told about a modern woman? What would she do with the box? You might enjoy composing some stories about modern-day gods and goddesses.

PROBING MORE

In fact, some "myths" about modern men and women have cropped up: the mythical "supermom" who tends the kids, keeps house, and holds down an important job at the office; or the "Mr. Mom" dad who stays home and does the housework while Mom works at the office. Think about the accuracy of these myths and what "truths" they are trying to get across. How does the supermom myth suggest the kind of roles that young women should grow up to play? How does the idea of a Mr. Mom helping out with housework set an example for young men?

There are hundreds of Greek and Roman myths you might enjoy reading. They're great yarns. You probably know some of them:

- Jason and the Argonauts retrieving the Golden Fleece
- Theseus tracking down the Minotaur in his labyrinth, then finding the way out with a skein of string he'd unraveled on the way in
- the Sirens, who sang to lure ships onto the rocks
- the one-eyed monster, Cyclops, tricked and slain by Ulysses
- snake-haired Medusa, whose looks turned people to stone

In case you'd like to read further, I have listed several good collections of mythological stories in the references for this chapter.

Myths and Legends in Our Time

Although we no longer imagine or worship gods and goddesses like those of the Greeks and Romans, there is still plenty of myth-and legend-making going on all around us. Myths and legends are a part of our lives.

For example, a morning newspaper reported, "Pigs Don't Litter!" Several readers of the *Detroit Free Press* had written to complain about a billboard slogan, *Don't Pig It Up, Pick It Up,* intended to keep people from littering the highways. Several pigs were pictured on the billboard.

"For centuries," wrote Denny Larke, "pigs have been the most maligned of animals," accused of being filthy and "piggish." Actually, he explained, "Pigs are exceptionally clean; they wallow in mud only to keep cool."

Barbara Schwartz wrote in to say: "This million-dollar ad scam once again perpetuates the myth of animals being inferior to humans, places more unnecessary blame on the innocent victims of man's cruelty, and relieves of responsibility the ones who create the problems."

In that letter, the word "myth" was used in the sense of a story that is false. It's important not merely to think about the "mistake" part of myths, but to see what they are trying to explain about the world and about human nature.

PROBING ON YOUR OWN

Myth and legend are in some ways in opposition to science, which insists on finding out the facts. Do pigs create litter or not? Are they a model of "piggishness" or not? You might be interested in checking out the facts behind some of these myths:
- Two-year-olds are terrible.
- Potatoes are fattening.
- When the *Titanic* sank, many men rushed to the lifeboats ahead of women and children. (Notice that this "unsinkable" ship was named after the Greek Titans!)
- Babe Ruth could call, beforehand, the exact pitch on which he would hit a home run and could point out the place where it would go over the wall.
- Woman's place is in the home.
- No two snowflakes are alike.

Television, comics, and the movies are constantly creating legends and myths. Just look at the "superheroes" and "superheroines"—Superman, Batman, Spider-Man, Wonder Woman, Iceman, Firelady, Robocop, the Dinoriders. These characters, decked out in their elaborate costumes, are modern-day gods and goddesses, endowed with superhuman powers. Sometimes this kind of myth gives us a chance to dream: Wouldn't life be nice if we could transform ourselves into invincible people whenever we got into a jam?

Science-fiction movies, too, have often shown mythical or legendary struggles between good and evil. *Star Wars,* probably the most famous of all sci-fi movies, clearly shows myth in action as a young good guy, Luke Skywalker, battles the forces of evil portrayed by the frightening Lord Darth Vader.

People who study myth and folklore have recently been especially interested in what they call "urban myths and legends." These are stories about everyday people, stories that are said to be true, stories that are passed on by word of mouth. The people who tell these tales believe they are true—sort of—even though nobody can actually verify that the story took place.

One common urban legend is one about a person who bought a bunch of bananas and was bitten by a tarantula lurking inside. Another is about someone finding a mouse inside a can of soda pop.

"The Babysitter" is an urban myth that was actually made into a film. It tells the story of a girl who receives threatening phone calls while she is baby-sitting at night. Eventually she has the call traced and is told by the operator that it is coming from within the house; a stranger, who turns out to be a killer, is on the second floor.

Almost as ghastly, and even more common, are myths about someone's pet that took a nap in a microwave oven and was zapped "until its eyes blew out."

What these stories are about—even the ones that involve fear and violence—is understanding the unknown. Just like the stories of ancient gods and goddesses, they help us understand some of life's mysteries, like where things came from, why there is evil, why people behave in odd and peculiar ways. Myths and legends are not science; they may even be wrong in their explanations; but they are a valuable and living way of helping us probe the unknown.

PROBING ON YOUR OWN

Myths and legends are being born around you all the time. Think about stories you've heard about teachers you may be studying with in a few years at a higher grade level. Are there "legendary" tough teachers or coaches at your school? Have you heard incredible stories about what happens in those classes? You might want to make a collection of such myths and legends, jotting them down, finding out just how true they are.

2

The Spirit World

From ghoulies and ghosties,
and long-leggedy beasties,
and things that go bump in the night,
O Lord, deliver us.

TRADITIONAL WELSH PRAYER

Things That Go Bump in the Night

There are many names for "creatures of the night," those dwellers in the spirit world that invade our lives and imaginations, that make ominous sounds at midnight, that lurk in dark shadows, and that provide the inspiration for millions of Halloween costumes. This chapter is about night creatures and "long-leggedy beasties," a list that includes:

ghosts	ghouls	goblins
spooks	manifestations	poltergeists
phantoms	brownies	fairies
gnomes	elves	genies
witches	warlocks	affrits
visitations	specters	vampires
werewolves	demons	gremlins

You may not actually believe in the existence of such creatures of the dark side, but you'll find evidence of their influence in everyday life, including our language:

"Now what in the devil made you do that?"

"There's a gremlin in my car and it just won't start."

Belief in a spirit world goes back to prehistory. Many mythological creatures had supernatural powers. There was Cyclops, the one-eyed giant who ate sailors for breakfast; the Minotaur, lurking inside a labyrinth and consuming sacrifices; even Pegasus, a magical winged horse.

In the 1500s, Martin Luther, a clergyman who led the Protestant Reformation, firmly believed in devils and reported that one pestered him as he worked on a translation of the Bible. On the other side of the globe, Hawaiian mythology contains stories of a Poison Word God, a spirit who, using words as a weapon, could actually pray people to death. Closer to home, curses such as "the devil with you" recall a time when people thought you really could call up the devil to cause pain for your enemies.

You have probably read Washington Irving's story "The Legend of Sleepy Hollow" or seen a TV version of it. Written just two hundred years ago, the story pokes fun at Ichabod Crane's belief in a spirit world. His terror causes him to run in fear at the sight of a "headless horseman." The ghost is actually one of Ichabod's enemies, who throws a pumpkin "head" at his victim. You may also be familiar with another Washington Irving story, "Rip Van Winkle," in which Rip, having slept for twenty years, awakes to find the ghosts of Henry Hudson and his crew bowling in the Catskill Mountains, making thunderous sounds.

Another famous spirit story is Scotsman Robert Burns's "Tam O'Shanter's Mare," in which Tam, a fun-loving guy whose courage is increased when he drinks a few beers, stumbles upon a meeting of witches. When they realize that a mortal is spying on them, the witches swarm out like a hive of angry bees. Tam escapes, but his horse, Meg, loses part of her tail, a reminder of a close encounter with the spirit world.

Claims of hauntings are common in our own time. Nigel Blundell and Roger Boar, who collect examples of spirit-world sightings, tell the story of what they call a "potatogeist" (a pun on "poltergeist"), a floating, headless figure who so terrified the night-shift workers at a potato-chip factory that an exorcist was called in to practice his special trade of scaring off ghosts.

Peter Underwood, a man who makes a career of investigating hauntings, reports:

> There is a particularly famous hotel in London which has a room in which a particularly unpleasant murder took place some years ago; whenever the room is occupied, the sounds of the murder are heard, the crime apparently being re-enacted, but without anything being visible. The room is never let, and if by chance you ask for it by number, you are always told that it is taken. It must be the most difficult hotel room in London to get into.

The Springport Inn of Harrisville, Michigan, is said to be haunted by the spirit of Joseph Van Buskirk, a lumberman who died over a century ago. The inn's owners, Pamela Lehr and Rebecca Stratton, say they never used to believe in ghosts until they bought the 111-year-old inn. Then strange things began to happen: Alarm clocks went off in the middle of the night; lights appeared in rooms where the sockets had no bulb; windows slammed shut and doors opened on their own; chairs moved in deserted rooms; tennis shoes mysteriously had their laces tied in knots.

"We laugh and joke about it and try to blow off these things," says Rebecca Stratton, "but Joseph doesn't go away. . . . I'm open-minded, and I feel comfortable here. We just know that someone's with us."

"We just know that someone's with us."

That chilling phrase sums up the feeling of many about the spirit world. You may even know of "haunts," places that are said to be the hangouts of ghosts, witches, spirits, goblins, or who knows what else. There may even be reports of hauntings in your own home-town.

PROBING ON YOUR OWN

If you're interested in learning about reports of hauntings in your area, ask your local librarian to help you find materials: They may be in a newspaper clippings file, or there may be some books written by hometown folks. Another place to check would be your local newspaper office, which probably has a library and may let you have a look through their files of haunting stories.

Often people can come up with explanations of peculiar or "ghostly" events: "Well, it must have been the wind." "Maybe the cat did it." Yet, most of us have had that thrilling, frightening feeling that *there's somebody or something out there.* It may be a long-leggedy or long-fanged creature. Perhaps it's a vampire waiting to lunch on us while we sleep. Maybe it's just the tooth fairy. But we have a hunch, as Stephen Larsen suggests, that the night creatures are running about, "prying open tombs, creeping through swamps and basements, hiding under your bed."

"No Monsters Under My *Bed." From "Professor Doodle" by Steve Sack and Craig MacIntosh. November 25, 1988.* Reprinted by permission of Tribune Media Services.

PROBING ON YOUR OWN

Have you ever had a "ghostly" encounter, a time when you saw something that might be a ghost or was certainly of a suspicious nature? What explanation do you have of this event? Or is it still unexplained in your mind? Interview other people: How many folks do you know who have had what they think might have been an encounter with the spirit world?

Creatures from the spirit world even come into the modern kitchen, at least according to Georgia Mae Lubeck of Oregon, who has written a book called *Ghost-Cooking*. She claims that a long-dead French chef named Jacques started hanging around her kitchen, offering her advice. The recipes he recommended were so delicious that she wrote them down. "This isn't a spooky experience," she says. "It's a creative experience."

As we'll see, many ghostly visitors are helpful and friendly, like Jacques, the French chef. On many cartoon shows, for example, the monsters, ghosts, pixies, and witches are harmless, sometimes even comical. The friendliest ghost of all was a comic book and cartoon character named Casper, whose big problem in the ghost world was that he didn't like to scare people.

PROBING ON YOUR OWN

I'll bet there've been many times when you thought there might be something under your bed or in the closet or upstairs in the dark. Or times when you heard noises that scared you and made you think there was somebody or something out there. Find a person who is interested in "things that go bump in the night" and compare your ghostly stories.

Most of the time we think of the spirit world with fear and trembling, not giggles and guffaws. Throughout history, people have taken the idea of ghosts and devils very seriously. Human beings suspected of being spirits have even been killed.

Three hundred years ago in New England descendants of the people who created the Thanksgiving celebration put to death a number of women who were thought to be witches. The Salem, Massachusetts, witch trials have gone down in history as a terrible example of what can happen when people fear the spirit world. Recently, scholars have suggested that the Salem witch hunt came about only because some teenage girls gossiped about possible witches in their midst and people in Salem believed them.

Ghost Stories

Just as the lion is the "king of beasts," the "big haunt" of the spirit world is your basic *ghost.*

"There are mad ghosts and wise ghosts," says Diana Norman, "bad ghosts, kindly ghosts, silly ghosts, protective ghosts—as many ghosts, in fact, as there are sides to human nature."

"The worst thing of ghosts," observes Philip Sergeant, "is that they refuse to be classified."

An amazing amount of folklore explains where ghosts come from, why they come back from the grave, what one can do in their presence. Looking at some of this lore, the stories and "knowledge" people have about ghosts, can give us ideas about why people persist in believing in these creatures from the unknown.

The general theory is that ghosts are the spirits of dead people who, for one reason or another, come back to "haunt" a familiar place. Haunting doesn't always mean frightening people or doing harm.

Christina Hole tells the story of a Dr. Jessop, a minister who, in the year 1879, was visited by a ghost that simply liked to hang around when Dr. Jessop was reading or writing. One night, having finished supper with friends, Dr. Jessop retired to his study. He explained:

> I had been engaged . . . about half an hour, and was just begin-
> ning to think my work was drawing to a close. As I was actually
> writing I saw a large white hand within a foot of my elbow.
> Turning my head, there sat a figure of a somewhat large man,
> with his back to the fire, bending slightly over the table, care-
> fully examining the pile of books I had been at work upon.

Dr. Jessop became convinced that the figure was not of this world. "There he sat, and I was fascinated, afraid not of his staying, but lest he should go." Eventually Dr. Jessop decided to resume his work, but when he reached for a book, the figure was startled and vanished.

There is no "natural" explanation of this story, no theory that the "ghost" might have been a curtain blowing in the breeze or a puff of smoke from the fireplace. Dr. Jessop himself worried that he had "lost his nerve" and was seeing things. He was concerned that it would look bad for a minister, a man of God, to report that he had seen a ghost. He went to bed puzzled and slept "the sleep of the just . . . or the guilty . . . I know not which."

Ghosts are more commonly connected with things evil. Dennis Bardens, who has written an "encyclopedia" of ghosts and hauntings (see the references for this chapter), reminds us that the author William Shakespeare wrote: "The evil that men do lives after them/The good is oft interred [buried] with their bones." Sometimes the "evil" that lives after people comes back to haunt them in the form of a ghost seeking revenge.

Dennis Bardens retells a two-thousand-year-old ghost story by Cicero, a famous Roman writer. There were two travelers: one stayed at a friend's house; the other stayed at an inn. During the night, the innkeeper murdered the second man and dumped his body in a cart, where it would be taken beyond the city walls and thrown out with the trash. However, in the middle of the night, the ghost of the murdered man appeared at the bedside of his friend, wakened him, and explained what had happened. The friend arose, located the cart, found the body, and was able to have the innkeeper imprisoned and punished by death for the murder.

The returning ghost is often a person who died in violent or terrifying circumstances, or sometimes the ghost is simply someone who died before all his life's work was finished. Ghosts are said to return from the grave to ask the living to finish a task or to correct a wrong or evil done to them or by them during their life.

You're probably familiar with one of the world's most famous and widely retold ghost stories: Charles Dickens's *A Christmas Carol.* There, the miserly, Christmas-hating Mr. Scrooge is warned to mend his ways by the ghost of his former partner, Jacob Marley. Because of Marley's own evil, he is doomed to pace the earth forever, dragging chains that he forged in life, each heavy link representing one of his miserly deeds. Warned by Marley and by three ghosts of Christmas past, present, and future, Scrooge vows to mend his ways. Of course, it turns out the ghosts were merely a dream. . . . Or were they?

PROBING ON YOUR OWN

You might enjoy swapping ghost stories that you've heard, perhaps while camping or on an overnighter with your friends. These stories are best told in a darkened room by flashlight, candlelight, or firelight: stories like "The Man with the Golden Arm" or "The Hook" or "The Claw" or even funny ones like the man who thought he saw a ghost at the foot of his bed, pulled out his gun, and shot himself in the big toe.

Some ghost experts suppose that even *events* have ghosts, leaving a "print" on the world. These events, usually occurrences of violence or great evil, repeat themselves from time to time—sort of a ghostly television replay. A ghost expert in London told me of the site of a bitter duel between two brothers, where grass won't grow in spots.

The bare patches are shaped like footprints, supposedly the footprints of the dueling brothers. It is also said that you can hear the sounds of the duel from time to time.

"The Far Side"
by Gary Larson.
Reprinted by permission
of Chronicle Features,
San Francisco, California.

"This is just not effective . . . We need to get some chains."

Of course, ghosts are not limited to people. *Animals* can haunt as well. Dogs have been said to come back to visit their masters and mistresses; so have cats, horses, and other kinds of animals.

But pigeons?

Christina Hole tells the story of some "pigeons of death," which were reported about the year 1700. It seems that a farmhouse in England was visited by a pair of pigeons about a week before a person in that house was going to die. Richard Gough, one of the owners of the farm, wrote about what happened before the death of his mother-in-law:

> The pair of pigeons came thither, which I saw. They did at
> every night roost under shelter of the roof of the kitchen. . . .
> In the daytime they flew about the gardens and the yards. I
> have seen them pecking . . . as if they did feed, and for all I
> know, they did feed.

Do "ghost pigeons" eat real food? Or do they just pretend to eat?
Do they eat Ghost Toasties?

How did Richard Gough conclude that these were *spirits,* not just
ordinary pigeons hanging around looking for a meal?

He became convinced because he had heard that the same pigeons
had been around before other deaths:

> My brother-in-law . . . feared his mother would die for there
> came such a pair of pigeons before his father's death, and he
> had heard they did so before the death of his grandfather.

About nine months later, the pigeons returned again, and there was
yet another death in the family, further convincing Mr. Gough that
they were visitors from the spirit world.

The ghost stories go on and on. They include stories about famous
people like Abraham Lincoln, the Queen of England, Harry
Houdini; legends of haunted castles, submarines, church towers; tales
of unexplained noises and mysterious lights coming from odd places;
rumors of faces at windows and people who appear and disappear at
odd times.

We have fewer reports of what it is like to actually *be* a ghost. We
know that Scrooge's partner, Marley, suffered in ghostdom and was
having no fun at all. Ghosts don't talk very much, but they are known
to moan and groan a great deal, suggesting that they can think of
happier places to be. A ghost's life, then, does *not* seem to be like
those in the cartoon world, where ghosts get to play pranks.

One description of life as a ghost is given by author Douglas
Adams, who, in his novel *Dick Gently's Holistic Detective Agency,*
writes about a brand-new ghost, a man who "wakes up" to discover
that he has died and become a *ghost*! "He tried standing up, slowly,

wonderingly, and wobblingly. The ground seemed to give him support. It took his weight. But then, of course, he appeared to have no weight that needed to be taken." The man/spirit's arms and legs felt rubbery. Although he could touch and vaguely feel objects in the physical world, he couldn't actually move things without a terrific effort. He began to learn the rules of ghostdom, that ghosts *can't* make just *anything* happen, that they can't interfere with human life any way they please. He managed to master the art of walking through solid doors, which, he reported, takes a lot of nerve the first time you try it.

PROBING ON YOUR OWN

What do you imagine life in the spirit world would be like? Is it a barrel of laughs or a time of pain and sadness? "Life As a Ghost" might be an interesting writing topic for you—for school or just for fun.

The Evidence for Ghosts and Other Spirits

There has always been debate over whether or not ghosts exist, a debate that goes on to this day. There are at least three groups of people who have taken a clear-cut stand on the issue of ghosts: the *believers,* the *nonbelievers,* and some folks I'll call the *ghostbusters.*

The Believers

Four hundred years ago, the philosopher John Locke, not a superstitious man given to quick judgments, argued in favor of creatures from the spirit world:

> That there should be more species of intelligent creatures above us than there are of sensible and material below us is probable to me. . . .

He argued that there are no "gaps" in nature from small creatures to large, from dumb creatures to the more intelligent. It therefore followed in his mind that the scale of life ought to just keep going into a ghostly spirit world, into the invisible domains.

Other believers have argued that just because we can't *see* ghosts is no reason to doubt them. As you probably know, the human eye is sensitive to only one band of light, the kind that lights up the world we see. There are other forms of light, like ultraviolet and infrared, that are invisible to us. Ghosts, it is argued, are like the invisible forms of light, surrounding us but not visible to ordinary human beings.

Some people claim to have a knack for seeing this invisible spirit world with a "third eye." Children, it is argued, possess this third eye more often than adults, because children are more open to new experiences than adults. Perhaps that explains why children, more than adults, are nervous about "things that go bump in the night." Maybe something *is* under the child's bed, something skeptical grown-ups just can't see!

Some believers say ghosts are part of a "fourth dimension." It takes special people to perceive this world, people who are psychic.

"If you are not psychic," writes Diana Norman, "ghosts can be fluttering thick as autumn leaves around you and you will be completely unaware of them."

T. C. Lethbridge, a believer, has even offered an explanation of ghosts as a form of electricity. He notes that our brains operate with tiny charges of electricity crossing nerve gaps, or synapses. Ghosts, says Mr. Lethbridge, are also basically electrical. But the human brain acts as a *resistance,* just as the cooking element on an electric stove creates a resistance to electrical current. Mr. Lethbridge claims that some people are able to lower that resistance so it becomes "relatively easy for their psycho-fields to act as a receiving set for projections on a similar wavelength." Thus for some folks, ghosts can be tuned in rather like a radio or TV broadcast!

Just as many religions have a belief in "life beyond the grave," many believers argue that human beings have "souls" that live on after physical death. Although people may stop breathing, their hearts may stop pumping, and their brains may show no activity, the soul does not die. Ghosts, then, are simply lost souls who haven't found their resting place.

The believers have made many efforts to prove the existence of ghosts "scientifically." Over one hundred years ago the Ghost Club was established to study the reports of hauntings. Although clear proof of ghosts has never been obtained, members of the club still track down reports of ghostly activity, hoping that someday solid proof will be found.

For the believers, there is no substitute for seeing a ghost for yourself. T. C. Lethbridge reports:

> My wife has recently seen a ghost and no longer treats me as being slightly simple for being interested in all this.

However, other ghost believers say that proof will never be found. Further, *they don't care.* They argue that ghosts are too busy being ghosts to fool around proving themselves to doubtful human beings who lack the third eye or who are not psychic and able to perceive things in the fourth dimension.

Diana Norman: "You cannot . . . prove ghosts to anyone who has never experienced them and does not want to believe in them."

Tom Cobett, a ghost chaser: "Ghosts cannot be put on the witness stand, or have their fingerprints taken. They are completely proof against proof."

The Nonbelievers

These people argue that belief in ghosts goes back to the Dark Ages, before the scientific method, when people were superstitious and believed that invisible forces controlled their lives. The nonbelievers feel that people are confused about the spirit world. When they see something they don't understand, they attribute it to ghosts or gremlins or even to mythological gods and goddesses. Further, the nonbelievers argue, most sightings or hauntings can be shown to have quite natural explanations.

For an example of a natural explanation of a haunting, one can turn to the world's most famous detective in literature, Sherlock Holmes, and the case of *The Hound of the Baskervilles*. This story shows what happens when people imagine there are ghosts on the prowl. In this celebrated case, the ghost is an animal: a dog, a "hound of hell." The famous detective and his sidekick, Watson, are called upon to solve the mystery of the death of Sir Charles Basker-ville. They keep hearing stories about a "monster" dog—the "Bas-kerville Demon"—that lives out on the moor. Many townspeople claim to have seen "a huge creature, ghastly and spectral."

The local doctor explains that Sir Charles died without a mark on his body, but with a look of sheer horror on his face. No human footprints were found near the body, but a little way off were "the footprints of a gigantic hound."

Holmes and Watson investigate and eventually wind up on the spooky moor in the dead of a foggy night. Sherlock Holmes appears to be unflappable, but Watson is nervous indeed, especially when he hears a great howl in the distance. Then something bursts through the fog:

> A hound it was, an enormous coal-black hound, but not such a hound as mortal eyes have ever seen. Fire burst from its open mouth, its eyes glowed with a smouldering glare, its muzzle and hackles and dewlap were outlined in flickering flame. Never in a delirious dream of a disordered brain could anything more sav-age, more appalling, more hellish be conceived than that dark form and savage face which broke upon us out of that wall of fog.

Watson is almost paralyzed with fear, but he recovers. He and Holmes pull out their revolvers and take shots at this "ghost." The bullets find their mark, and when it is all finished, they discover a

The Hound of the Baskervilles, a drawing from Strand Magazine *(February, 1902), in which the story was first published.*

huge but mortal dog that had been covered with phosphorus to make it glow in the dark.

Sherlock Holmes determines that some men who wanted Sir Charles Baskerville dead created this glowing beast and literally frightened him to death.

You can see from Watson's dramatic description what must have happened. In the darkness, dreadfully nervous, he exaggerated the image of that hound in his mind until it appeared much more frightening than it was.

Writing an introduction to this Sherlock Holmes story, novelist John Fowles tells of another hound that is to be found in his hometown. It is actually a very little dog, he says, but at night as that pup follows you down a lonely alley, your impressions of its size grow until it seems "as big as a bull when it finally slavers over you, ready for the kill." Imagination, not ghosts, has turned a harmless dog into a creature of the night.

Nonbelievers point out that ghosts tend to show up most often when people are unhappy or tired or alone or frightened, times when they may not be thinking too carefully or when they are, like Watson and Sir Charles Baskerville, likely to be persuaded to believe in things that go bump in the night.

PROBING ON YOUR OWN

Think about rumors and legends and how they grow, including scary things that become more and more frightening as people talk about them. Recall a time when your own imagination ran wild and turned something into a real nightmare. You'll get a sense of how ghost stories can grow from natural events.

Some nonbelievers even point out that people often *enjoy* being scared. Why else would people ride roller coasters or seek out the "demon drop" at the county fair? Why would they go to movies about monsters that haunt Elm Street or watch late-night TV, where vampires and ghouls are likely to give them bad dreams? Because life is an unknown, because we don't know what's out there in the dark, we sometimes like to test ourselves with "affrights." It may be that ghost sightings are a variation of playing with some of the fearsomeness of the unknown.

We also need to consider the fact that ghosts may be "real" in an imaginary sense. That is, although ghosts may not exist as actual spirit creatures, the *idea* of ghosts itself can be very real in people's minds. When a person dies, for example, the living people retain a memory of him or her. That memory is something like a ghost or spirit. It's common to hear that the "ghost" of a relative has influenced how people live and act. Or you've heard that one can almost feel the "spirit" of Grandma or Grandpa at a family gathering. The memory of a person who has died can thus remain behind to "haunt" us. But, the nonbelievers insist, ghostly memories are certainly not proof of creatures from the dark side.

The Ghostbusters

In between the believers and nonbelievers are the people I'll call ghostbusters—after the film and cartoon shows that have been popular in recent years. Ghostbusters are believers but feel that mortals can *control* the spirit world. An exorcist is a person said to have the power to banish spirits that have invaded the body of a living person. Ghostbusters also go under the names of *shaman, witch doctor,* and *sorcerer.*

In some parts of the world witch doctors recite chants and use combinations of herbs to rid sick people of the evil spirits that are causing them pain. Sorcerers and shamans cast spells and brew up potions to aid the sick or to exorcise evil from people and places.

Whether you think ghostbusters are really accomplishing something depends, in large measure, on whether you're a believer or nonbeliever in the spirit world. If you believe spirits are "out there," then you will probably also believe in the powers of the ghostbuster.

If you're not persuaded that spirits exist, you might be reminded of the old joke about the man who said he could scare away *elephants.* It goes like this:

> Once a child who liked to play in the park saw a man sitting on a park bench, tearing a newspaper into tiny little strips, and scattering them around.
> "What are you doing?" asked the child.
> "Scaring off the elephants," replied the man.
> "But there are no elephants around here," the child asserted.
> "I guess my method works!" exclaimed the man.

Obviously if a ghostbuster is practicing his or her art and you don't see any ghosts, you have proof of two different kinds. The believer says, "See, it works!" The nonbeliever snorts and says, "Yeah, but there aren't any ghosts around in the first place. Or elephants either."

Other Creatures That Go Bump in the Night

To open this chapter, I listed some of the many inhabitants of the spirit world. Some of these are regular "performers" on television and in the movies.

Werewolves

These creatures grew from the folklore of Europe, where reports of them have circulated for centuries. Werewolves are human beings that turn into killer wolves under special circumstances, usually the light of a full moon. In some folktales they look like hairy men, walking upright. In other stories they look exactly like wolves. Ghostbusters know that to kill a werewolf, you have to shoot it with a silver bullet.

Vampires

Vampires are night creatures, usually the restless and wandering souls of people who were especially evil in life. As you no doubt know, vampires have sharp, hollow incisor teeth and suck the blood of their victims, leaving two little puncture marks on the neck. It is said that you can detect a vampire because it casts no shadow and has no reflection in a mirror. The time-honored method of destroying a vampire is to find its resting place, which will be a coffin in some dark place where sunlight cannot penetrate. While the vampire is asleep, drive a stake through its heart. Or open up the coffin lid, then the windows, and let the sun shine in; the light will destroy it. Or sneak into the vampire's "home" at night while it's on the prowl and steal the coffin, leaving it no resting place. However, folklore says that some vampires prepare several coffins in different places just to thwart such a scheme.

To Believe or Not to Believe: That's the Question

Scientific investigation has never presented proof of the spirit world; yet, as we've seen, belief in ghosts, goblins, and night creatures continues. And vampires, gremlins, and ghoulies do a thriving business on television and in the movies. Like the gods, goddesses, and creatures in myths and legends, beings from the spirit world offer a tempting explanation of the mysteries we confront in life. Like mythical and legendary characters, however, ghosts and spirits present only one kind of explanation of the unknown. We'll look at other explanations in the chapters to come.

3

Superstition and Folkways

One of the scariest Greek myths tells of three sisters: Clotho, Lachesis (Lah-*key*-sis), and Atropos (Ah-*troh*-pos). They are better known as the Fates. They spin out a thread representing the life of every mortal on earth. The sisters also are equipped with a pair of scissors, and when a person's time is up, they snip the thread. The Fates, in short, are said to determine when we human beings are to die.

The Fates are not a kindly trio. The Roman poet Catullus described them as "decrepit," with "tottering bodies" that sway as they wield their deadly scissors. They are cruel and unrelenting in taking human lives.

One tragic myth tells the story of Admetus (Ad-*mee*-tus), a suitor for the hand of the lovely Alcestis (Al-*ses*-tis). Admetus became gravely ill, and he beseeched the Fates to let him live longer. They agreed but demanded another human life to take in exchange. Admetus asked his friends if one of them would take his place in death, but there were no volunteers. Seeing no one step forward, Alcestis herself volunteered; she would die so that her lover might live. As Admetus recovered, the Fates took the life of Alcestis, clipping her thread too early in life.

Times have changed, of course. Nowadays a girl would be a lot less

"The Fates." Note that one of the Three Sisters has stretched out the thread of someone's life while a second has scissors ready to snip it off in the middle. Florence, Galleria Pitti. Alinari/Art Resource.

likely to die for her boyfriend. But the myth of Admetus and Alcestis demonstrates how the fear of the unknown—of the Great Unknown, death—can drive human beings to do strange and even brave things.

Control over death was not the only power given to the Fates. As their name suggests, their threads controlled life as well, and your future—your fate—was spun out in your thread, like a computer program for the future or perhaps like a chromosome with all your future traits embedded in it.

The Fates themselves would sometimes offer predictions. Before the battle of Troy, they predicted the death of the great hero Achilles (Ah-*kill*-eez). At his birth, Achilles' mother had dunked him in the river Styx (Sticks), and that had supposedly made him invulnerable: He could not be wounded. Therefore at Troy he ignored the warning of the Fates and went into battle anyway. Unfortunately for him, nobody had told him that his mother had held him by the heel when dunking him, and that part of his body was not protected. An arrow shot from the walls of Troy found its mark—Achilles' heel—and he died as the Fates had prophesied. From that story, of course, we get the expression "Achilles' heel," which means a weak spot, a place where you can be hurt or wounded easily.

Superstition and Soothsayers

> When lighting flashed and thunder roared across vale and mountain in ancient times, our ancestors petitioned favours of Oden, most powerful of the Norse gods, and omniscient [all-knowing] ruler of heaven and earth. Whether in Britain or Gaul, Sweden or Norway, while ordinary folk in their rude huts and shelters quaked in fear of the elements, the wise ones stood on high cliffs and ledges, faces white with ecstasy, bodies bedecked with bones and painted with symbols, to hear the wishes and instructions of the gods or to try to direct lesser spirits themselves.

So writes Raymond Lamont Brown, dramatically describing how soothsayers and fortune predictors have held power in the minds of people. Human beings have always wanted to know about the future and have turned to people who claim to be able to predict it. Throughout history you'll find stories about soothsayers and fortune tellers, shamans, prophets, oracles, and, of course, Fates.

The scene changes: We're no longer watching an ancient soothsayer on a high cliff taunting a storm and trying to discover the secrets of Fate. We're at a basketball game in the present-day United States.

The score is tied; we're near the end of the game. A player is fouled. He or she steps to the foul line, bounces the ball exactly five times, takes a deep breath, and shoots. The ball bounces away from the rim. The shooter steps back, carefully moving outside the foul circle, looks away from the basket, walks back to the line, bounces the ball exactly five times, takes a deep breath, and shoots. The ball goes in the basket, and the shooter's team continues on to victory. (By the way, our hero/ine has not changed socks since the team began its winning streak!)

Question: How many times do you think the shooter will bounce the ball the *next* time he or she goes to the line? And those socks: Will they be thrown in the laundry this week?

Superstition involves doing something by custom or habit because you think it helps controls the future. Carrying a rabbit's foot for good luck or refusing to walk under a ladder for fear of bad luck are both superstitious acts. Many modern people like to think that they're not superstitious.

However, many people have more superstition in them than they recognize or admit. For example, you can find some interesting connections between the way our basketball player handled those foul shots and the way the Greeks and others consulted ancient soothsayers and fortune tellers. Our basketballer probably didn't stand on a mountaintop the night before the big game or prepare a sacrifice to the gods. In fact, to the contrary, the team's coach may well have warned the players, "Your *fate* is in your own hands tonight."

However, the coach may also have advised: "Always do the same thing when you go to the foul line. That way, when you're under pressure, you can perform steadily."

"Take a deep breath before shooting; that will help you relax," the coach might have said. "And bounce the ball once or twice to relax your arms."

Okay, so our player was following the coach's advice, not being superstitious. At first.

But what about exactly *five* bounces? What about stepping *outside* the foul ring after a missed shot? Above all, what about those filthy, smelly, stick-to-the-wall-where-you-throw-them socks? Parts of our basketballer's ritual look rather superstitious. That is, they are done simply because the player did them in the past, and things worked. There is no *evidence* that the ritual put the ball in the basket, but, what the heck, we did it this way in the past, so we might as well keep on.

Can a pair of dirty socks bring about a winning streak? Probably not, but our basketballer doesn't want to "tempt fate" by changing them. Is there anything special about bouncing the ball five times (as opposed to three or seven)? Probably not, but we'll keep on using five bounces unless we hit an "unlucky streak," and then perhaps the "magic" number will be changed.

Is It in the Stars?

Most daily newspapers carry a feature called the horoscope. Often you'll find it listed on the front page contents, right along with news, sports, weather, comics, and the television page. A horoscope consists of advice about how to live, based on astrology, the art of predicting the future using the stars as a guide.

According to astrologers, the positions of the stars and planets at the moment of birth affect the kind of person you will be and what your life will be like. Stars, rather than the Fates, hold the power of the future. Your astrological sign is a constellation prominent in an imaginary belt of stars called the zodiac. If you were born between

January 20 and February 18, for example, your zodiac sign is Aquarius. As an Aquarian, you are said to be a mellow sort of person. On the other hand, if you were born between December 22 and January 19, you're a Capricorn, born under the sign of the goat, and you are predicted to be more feisty and aggressive.

In addition to the forces of the stars and planets at your birth, astrologers also believe that the daily positions of the heavenly bodies influence your life pattern. Thus they write the daily horoscopes that appear in the newspaper.

The horoscope offers daily advice based on your birth sign. A typical daily horoscope might read like this:

> **Capricorn** (December 22 to January 19). Beware of your stubborn tendencies. Now is the time to be charming.
>
> **Aquarius** (January 20 to February 18). Do not be hasty in the work you are completing. Be your relaxed self. Time will be on your side.

Astrologers and their work are very controversial. Many people regard astrology as pure superstition. It's a fake and a fraud, they say, a "pseudo," or make-believe, science. Yet a surprising number of people throughout history have taken astrology seriously. Adolf Hitler, the German dictator, delayed military operations until the stars were "right" (and actually lost key battles because of his dependency on astrologers, for which his opponents thanked their lucky stars).

Even though entire books have been written showing that astrology doesn't work (see the references listed for this chapter), millions of people around the world read horoscopes daily, and many of them follow the dictates of the stars. Hundreds of newspapers wouldn't print daily horoscopes if people weren't reading them for one reason or another.

Part of the trick of horoscopes is that they are written in very vague language. Suppose your horoscope advises, "This is a good day to consult with friends." How could it go wrong? *Every* day you consult with friends, and so there is a possibility for developing important relationships with them. Or suppose you read that "today you will make key decisions." How many days *don't* you make important decisions of one kind or another? As R. F. Smith has argued, "Astrology works backward. It begins with a conclusion, then forces as many facts as possible to fit it, discarding the rest." What he's saying, then, is that you can *always* find some facts or events in your life that fit today's prediction.

Astrology believers argue back: "The stars impel, they do not compel." They explain the vagueness of horoscopes by saying these are general, not exact, predictions so that the horoscope user must take responsibility for figuring out the applications in his or her own life. Just as there was some flexibility in the futures predicted by the Fates, so there's opportunity for a person to shape his or her own fate within the forces of the stars.

PROBING ON YOUR OWN

Francis Bacon, a British writer and philosopher, once said, "In all superstition wise men follow fools."

Where do you stand on superstition? Do you see yourself as superstitious? Do you have a lucky number? Any lucky clothing? Do you avoid black cats? Do you try not to walk under a ladder? Are there any special patterns that you follow in school or in sports? You may find that you have some harmless superstitions—some things you don't really believe in but do anyway. Still, it's good to know what your superstitions are.

Interview some of your parents, friends, teachers, and coaches on the question of superstition. Chances are, you'll find some people who claim, "I'm not superstitious!" but who do practice some bits of superstitious behavior.

Interestingly enough, Francis Bacon also said, "There is superstition in avoiding superstition." What do you suppose he meant by that?

PROBING ON YOUR OWN

Study your own horoscope and see what you think. Clip the horoscope column from the daily newspaper for a week or more, and each day jot down facts in your life that do or do not fit the prophesy. What do you conclude?

As an additional experiment, study the horoscope for a *different* sign than your own, and see whether it applies to you. That is, if you're an Aquarian, pretend you're a Capricorn. Does the advice to the goat people apply to your life too?

Before one condemns astrology as mere superstition, it is important to recognize that it had its origins in a true science, that of *astronomy,* which has the same Latin root word, *astrum,* meaning "star."

Three to four thousand years ago, during the early years of recorded history, people studied the stars and used them for navigation and agriculture. They recognized that certain star patterns tended to be in the same part of the sky at the same time each year, giving the sailor a reliable target for navigating and the farmer a reliable guide to managing crops.

Twenty-eight hundred years ago, the Greek poet Hesiod gave this advice based on the constellations of the Pleiades (*Plee*-ah-deez), a small cluster of stars also called the Seven Sisters, and Orion, the constellation also known as the Hunter:

> Begin your harvest when the Pleiades are rising
> and your plowing when they are setting. . . .
> Winnow grain when powerful Orion first appears. . . .

This was not superstition, but early science.

An example of how *astronomy* turned into *astrology* is recorded by another Greek, a writer named Plutarch, who called the star Sirius

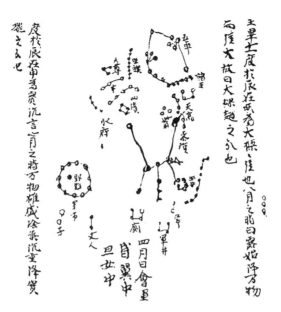

This diagram of the constellation Orion was drawn 1500 years ago by a Chinese astronomer. Although the observation was made on the side of the globe opposite North America, it shows a pattern of stars familiar to any North American stargazer. From a manuscript found in Tunhuang by Sir Aurel Stein. Courtesy of the British Library.

the "bringer of the Nile." He observed that, in Egypt, the Nile river usually overflowed when Sirius was prominent in the heavens. People concluded, wrongly, that Sirius was the *cause* of the flooding (the bringer of the Nile), not just a star that showed up at the same time as the floods.

Remembering that people were still living in the age of myth and fully believed in spirits, it's easy to see, then, how people made false connections among the gods, the natural world, and star patterns.

Thus astrology grew. As people passed on ideas and customs from generation to generation, and as seers and soothsayers and fortune tellers tried to satisfy people's fear of the unknown, astrology became more and more popular and retains its powerful hold on many people today.

The Amazing World of Futurology

Futurology—the art of predicting the future—has taken many forms over thousands of years. Fortune tellers, seers, and oracles of all kinds have looked for signs of the future in an incredible number of ways. They have gazed into crystal balls and studied tea leaves in a cup. They have even baked animal bones and studied the patterns of cracks for a "map" of the future.

Over one hundred fifty years ago, Charles Mackay wrote a wonderful book called *Extraordinary Popular Delusions and the Madness of Crowds,* in which he analyzed the forms of fortune telling. The names of many of these techniques all end in the suffix *-mancy,* which means "divining" or "predicting." For example, fortune tellers have practiced:

- *ornithomancy,* studying flights of birds;
- *icthyomancy,* examining fish behavior;
- *aeromancy,* looking to the winds and weather for clues to the future.

Now, with those three forms of fortune telling, you can see that there might be some connections between the natural world and predicting. If birds fly south early in the autumn, you might suppose there is a hard winter coming. If fish show odd patterns of behavior, say, showing up in large numbers or not showing up at their usual time, you might suppose that a drought or flood may be pending.

In our own time, we engage in what might be called wooly-bear-caterpillar-mancy when we predict a hard winter if the middle stripe of a caterpillar is extra wide.

More "-mancies"

Name	Fortune Telling by Studying
idolmancy	idols or statues and images
botanomancy	flowers

lithomancy	stones
oneiromancy	dreams
onychomancy	fingernails
tephromancy	ashes
catoptromancy	mirrors
chartomancy	writing
capnomancy	a skull filled with smoke

Crystalomancy, as you might suppose, involved using a crystal ball to see into the future. *Astralogomancy* used rolls of the dice to look for number combinations. A very popular form of fortune telling in China, still practiced today, is *I Ching,* which involves tossing coins or maneuvering stalks from the yarrow plant to find significant number combinations that are said to predict the future. Like horoscopes, *I Ching* predictions are phrased in vague language that lets a person make his or her own decisions. Richard Smith says its predictions are like the advice of "a kindly but shrewd uncle with a rich store of sensible and normally safe advice."

Chiromancy, or *palmistry,* remains another popular form of fortune telling. You can have your palm read at a county fair (or sometimes, for fun, at a school fair). The claim of palmistry is that the shape of your hand and the lines on it give an indication of your future. In particular, the life line, which runs across your palm, gives a clue about how long you will live (or when the three Fates will snip your thread).

Palm reading is often linked to mythology and astrology. There is the Mound of Jupiter on your hand, and mounds of Saturn, Apollo, Mercury, and Venus, along with a Plain of Mars, each with its own significance. In some systems of palm reading, each of the three joints of your four fingers (count them, there are twelve) stands for one of the twelve signs of the Zodiac, so your hand represents a miniature astrological system. On the basis of your palm, then, a palmist can offer very general predictions about your ambition, love life, temperament, "gloomth" or happiness, and many other human traits.

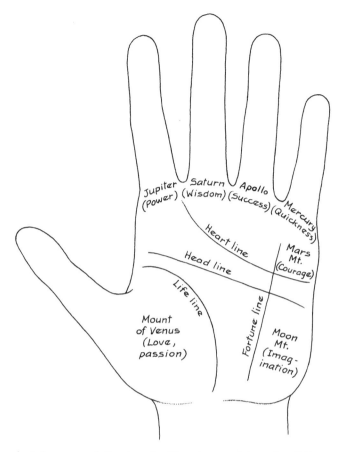

A palmist's map of the hand. The size and length of lines and "mounts" (mounds) give the palmist clues to a person's future and basic nature. The life line indicates how long one is expected to live. The length of the heart, head, and fortune lines supply clues to passions, intellect, and prospects for success. The mounts, which are named after the moon and various planets, represent the characteristics of the mythological gods whose names they carry.

Does palmistry work? The modern thinker has to be doubtful. However, at least one present-day palm reader, Fred Gettings, reminds us that our hands often reveal signs of the kind of work we do. He claims that modern palmistry takes that into account. If you've ever read books about the fictional detective Sherlock Holmes, you know that he could tell all kinds of things about people, including their emotions, by studying their hands. As a detective, you might predict that a person who has rough, callused hands will work hard in the future, that someone with chewed fingernails will be nervous under stress. Even though you don't want to fall into superstitious behavior, you can see that palms might offer a clue to a person's past or future.

PROBING ON YOUR OWN

Fortune telling is a fascinating and complicated topic, and I can only begin to touch on its details in this chapter. If you're interested in learning more, head for the library. Several helpful books are listed in the references for this chapter. In addition, check the subject catalog for some of the following topics:

Tarot (fortune-telling cards)

Palmistry (reading palms)

Augury (studying omens or "signs")

Necromancy (communicating with the spirit world)

or

Invent a make-believe fortune-telling scheme of your own, complete with a name. Consider:

Name	*Fortune Telling by*
sneakermancy	studying wear and tear on shoes
lunchomancy	predicting what people like to eat
teachermancy	guessing what your teacher is going to do to you next

---

Superstitious Objects and Charms

For reasons that are often lost in history or memory, objects sometimes become the center of superstitious behavior.

In Gloucestershire, England, for example, people would sometimes wear a chunk of grass and its attached dirt under their hats to ward off bad luck and evil spirits. Also in England, Saint Thomas

Aquinas was said to have buried a small bronze horse in the center of the road outside his house. That, in turn, scared away horses and riders who were disturbing his study. There are all kinds of "lucky" objects: rabbits' feet, coins, four-leaf clovers. Often these are objects that people link with a good time in life, objects such as a lucky pebble found at a good day at the beach, or a lucky pop-bottle cap found the day somebody got a good mark in a test, or a lucky pair of socks somebody wore as long as his or her basketball team was winning.

Stones have a strong superstitious history. There are witch stones (to keep away evil spirits), holy stones (to attract favorable spirits), adder stones (which are said to cure snakebites), and toad stones (small, "warty"-looking rocks that help keep away evil). Stones that have holes in them, created by water over centuries of time, are said to be lucky, and often the finder will put a string or leather thong through the hole and wear the stone as a necklace or a charm. Good luck "breeding stones" are said to help women or animals have babies; these are found in the fields in springtime after the winter freeze has brought a new crop of rocks to the surface, making it look as if the field has had babies.

And let's not forget the "pet rock" fad in the United States. A smart merchandiser started selling ordinary stones as pets. People became quite attached to their stones, giving them names, consulting them for advice (if your stone doesn't answer, it probably is saying no), even imagining that the stone had moods. Although the "pet rock" phenomenon was a joke, people started to treat their "pets" superstitiously.

You may know of birthstones, one for each month of the year, which, like your zodiac birth sign, are said to reflect or determine your personality traits:

Month/Stone	Traits
January/ garnet	constancy
February/amethyst	sincerity

March/aquamarine — courage
April/diamond — innocence
May/emerald — success in love
June/pearl or agate — health and long life
July/ruby — contentment
August/ sardonyx — faithfulness
September/sapphire — reasonableness
October/opal — hope
November/topaz — loyalty
December/turquoise — prosperity

PROBING ON YOUR OWN

Compare your personality type as predicted by the stars (your zodiac sign) with the prediction of your birthstone. Do you find any connection? If they differ, which one, if either, would you trust?

or

Look around and find yourself a nice pet rock. Test out its behavior.

Often lucky or superstitious objects can be linked to mythology. The lucky horseshoe, for example, is traced to a tale of Saint Dunstan, a blacksmith, who was being vexed by the devil. In mythology and folklore, the devil often has a cloven hoof, like a goat. This particular devil needed a new shoe for his hoof and came to Dunstan. The good blacksmith tricked the devil into standing against a wall, then pinned him there with a horseshoe and nails. The devil was released only after promising to be a good boy. The devil hasn't kept that promise, of course, but he won't enter a place where a horseshoe is hung, either. Another myth says that horseshoes are lucky because witches are frightened of horses, and a horseshoe over your door keeps witches at bay.

Let's not forget lucky numbers as we discuss superstition. The number one has been said to be lucky because of its "wholeness," since it cannot be divided into other whole numbers. Three is a superstitious number from way back and appears in many forms, sometimes as a sign of good luck, sometimes as an omen of evil: the three Fates, three wishes, three cheers. It's interesting that in a great many stories, things happen in threes, as in the "Three Little Pigs," where it's the third house (of brick) that withstands the wolf's attack. Seven is a lucky number because of seven stars in the Big Dipper and the Pleiades. There are seven major virtues (faith, hope, charity, justice, prudence, temperance, fortitude), and there are seven deadly sins (pride, greed, waste, envy, piggishness, rage, and laziness).

Thirteen is the all-time unlucky number. Several myths trace this number back to Norse mythology, where Loki, the trickster, was the thirteenth person and a party crasher at a banquet where the god Balder was slain. Christians note that thirteen people were present at the Last Supper on the night before Jesus was slain. Thirteen has such powerful superstitious traits that many buildings do not have a thirteenth floor; you just go from twelve to fourteen.

Household Superstitions and Folkways

The list of superstitions goes on and on. People are superstitious about:

Spilling salt, which is said to bring bad luck. If you spill some, superstition says you should toss a pinch of it over your left shoulder, where the devil is said to lurk.

Colors: In our culture blue is said to be "true" and yellow the color of cowardice. Red is often associated with blood and death, and with hot-tempered redheads. White symbolizes purity, and black is the traditional color of the forces of night and evil. Purple is royal, and so on.

Spitting! In some lands, fishermen spit on their nets for good luck. In other places, it's good luck to spit when you enter a place of danger.

PROBING ON YOUR OWN

Many people feel that number superstitions are some of the worst kinds, because we *know* that there cannot be any direct connection between a number—which is just a symbol, after all—and things that happen in the real world. Nevertheless, most people have feelings about numbers. You might want to talk to people to learn their beliefs. Do they have special numbers? Do they use these numbers, say, in picking a lottery ticket?

If you're interested in one way of "discovering" a lucky number, just for fun, not superstition, here's a formula. I'll show you the calculation for my own birthdate, January 31, 1942:

1) Add together: The day of your birth, the month of your birth (as a number, 1 to 12), and the year of your birth. You'll get a four-digit number. [For me the calculation is 31 + 1 + 1942 = 1974]

2) Add those four numbers together. You'll come up with a two-digit number. [1 + 9 + 7 + 4 = 21]

3) Add those two digits to find your lucky number. [2 + 1 = 3]

(Whoops! When I was young, I thought 7 was my lucky number. I always wore it on my basketball uniform. Maybe if I'd switched to 3 I would have gone on to be a hoop star.)

Mirrors, especially breaking one, which causes you to "shatter" an image of yourself.

As I have suggested, however, often there is a grain of truth associated with a superstition. Breaking a mirror certainly isn't *good* luck. Superstitions regarding salt are said to date to a time when salt was a precious spice and spilling it was costly. (But then why would you toss some over your shoulder?)

Sometimes the truth is more than just a grain, and what looks like superstition becomes a custom or a practice that people follow because it works. We call such practices folkways.

For example: One morning before heading off for school, you check the weather. You could turn on the radio and get a forecast. Instead, you stick your head out the door, see that the sky is gray, and say:

> Cloudy and gray,
> raincoat today.

Without thinking further, you stuff a raincoat in your bookbag and head out the door.

Is this superstition? You don't know where the rhyme came from. Although it might resemble consulting the stars or reciting a chant, actually this is a folkway that has been in your family for years. You keep using it because it's a pretty reliable way of going about keeping dry. (If instead of carrying a raincoat you said, "I'll just cross my fingers for luck," *that* would be superstition.)

In societies all over the world, customs like the raincoat rhyme are passed on from one generation to another. Folkways are usually passed on by word of mouth, but you'll find many of them written down. A good source of folkways is the almanac, a guidebook to practical life.

The most famous almanac in America is one that was published by Benjamin Franklin over two hundred fifty years ago. In *Poor Richard's Almanack,* Franklin tried "to inform his readers of numerous intelligences, most especially on the future and the vagaries of the weather." Ben Franklin was not a superstitious person, and he concentrated on giving practical advice, such as his famous "A penny saved is a penny earned." But as almanacs developed, they became interesting collections of folklore, superstition, and science. The modern *Old Farmer's Almanac,* for example, contains articles on such topics as beauty tips, unusual things to do with vinegar, how to hypnotize a lobster, how to control weeds in the garden, and why molasses is good for you, as well as a guide to consumer purchasing.

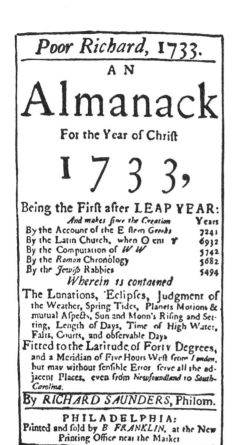

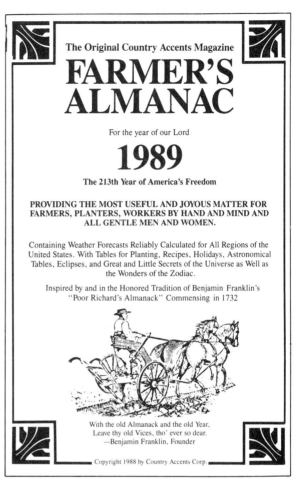

Poor Richard's Almanack *and a modern almanac.* Title page of *Farmer's Almanac* reprinted by permission of GCR Publishing Group.

The almanac also contains horoscopes and an "astronomical" prediction of the weather based on a "secret formula." It is fascinating to study the advertisements in the almanac, too; there you'll find people selling personalized fortunes, the secrets of witchcraft, and fortune-telling cards.

One article presents ways of curing warts:

> Dead cats, mashed ants, dandelion juice, chicken feet, dirt from a fresh grave—they're all good for curing warts. You can talk them off, hypnotize them away, wish them on a gray

horse's backside, or lick them every morning until they disappear. There are probably more folk remedies for warts than for any other complaint, and the amazing thing is that they all work—*if* you believe them.

In collecting folk cures for warts, Tim Clark found over fifty. Study his list and see if you can figure out where and how these might have originated.

PROBING ON YOUR OWN

Most families have a number of folkways. Some of these are mere superstitions; others are just traditional ways of doing things. They may have to do with curing disease, preparing food, getting work done in the yard or around the house. How do people in your family go about curing the hiccups, for example? What (if anything) do they believe about curing warts? What do they believe is the best way to raise children or pets? Your family may have its own collection of "lucky" objects. You might be interested in making a study of your family's folkways, perhaps even putting them down in a notebook to save. Begin by interviewing your parents, but if possible, go to your grandparents or other older family members as well.

Why Superstitions and Folkways Persist

As you can see, folkways, customs, traditions, and superstitions often do have their roots in the "truth," and if you look hard enough, you can find a logical reason for them. At the same time, many superstitions clearly don't work, and the reasons for following many folkways have been forgotten. Horoscopes don't do an especially accurate job of predicting the future any more than breaking a mirror or walking under a ladder invariably brings bad luck. Warts *might* go away if you follow the folkway and rub them with lemon juice (which contains a mild acid and would therefore possibly dissolve a wart), but if you rub your wart with a chicken foot, good luck to you (and the chicken).

Why do people keep doing things that work only some of the time, if at all?

In some cases, it's simply that people know superstition or a folkway doesn't really work, but they figure there's no harm in it. For example, except for offending other people, a basketball player who wears the same socks for weeks doesn't do any harm.

It also turns out that folkways are a pretty good way to teach young people what you want them to do without their having to ask questions. If you have memorized your family's raincoat rhyme, you will seldom go out without protection from the rain. As children are born into the world, their families need to teach them how the world works, and folkways can be a way of doing that. *Never go out on a dark and stormy night* may sound like a superstition but may be just a plain good rule to follow when lightning is flashing. *Don't fool around with electricity* is another bit of advice that makes electricity sound almost magical, but may simply be a way of keeping kids from electrocuting themselves.

However, there can also be harm in following superstition and folkways thoughtlessly. You can get yourself into trouble if you "follow the stars" blindly, without making decisions on your own. And some folk remedies, such as picking at a wart until it bleeds, can actually be harmful.

In the end, the reasons for the persistence of superstition and folkways can be traced back to anxiety about the unknown world. As the Fates have shown us, we don't know what's going to happen to us next, and that's a scary prospect. We want some *control* in our lives. Through ritual, custom, superstition, and folkways, people get a little reassurance for themselves.

4

Magic and Illusion

Stare at the figure shown here for a few seconds. Look closely at the points where the white lines meet. Most people see tiny gray squares at those junctions. They will be faint but seem real. Where did they come from?

This checkerboard is called the Hermann Grid. It's an illusion that is created by the sharp contrast of black on white coupled with the tendency of the eye to hold afterimages. Our brains also like to "fill in the blanks," seeing complete patterns rather than empty spaces.

Put all those together and you have the Hermann Grid illusion—
"real" gray squares that aren't there at all.

Sometimes school science books show the eye as being like a camera: An image passes through a lens in the eye and is recorded on "film" (the retina) at the back of the eye. But this comparison is not completely accurate. In contrast to a camera, the eye is "wired" to the brain by way of the optic nerve. It's in the brain that "seeing" takes place, and the brain is not at all like a piece of film. The brain *thinks* and it *interprets* the images that flow into it.

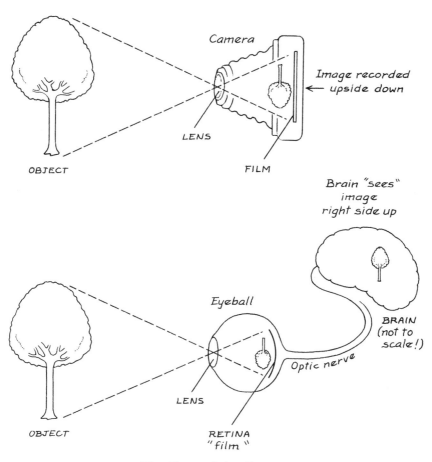

The Eye and the Camera

In the last century, a British psychologist, G. M. Stratton, had some hunches about how the brain helps the eye interpret images. He reasoned that the eye, like a camera, actually produces an upside-down image in the eyeball, because the image "crosses over" as it passes through the lens. (See the X-shaped lines on the sketch.) Yet we see things right side up! Stratton believed that our brains flip-flop the image for us in order to match the world we know is out there. To prove this, he gave some people, the subjects of his experiment, glasses that were made out of optical prisms. These glasses actually turned the image upside down before it entered the eye. Therefore when the lens of the eye turned the image end for end, the image was landing on the back of the eyeball right side up. What did people see? *They saw the world upside down.* If that's confusing, check the diagram of Stratton's experiment.

Stratton's subjects were still automatically reversing the image in their minds. However, after the subjects got used to the glasses, they started seeing the world right side up again! Their brains adapted the incoming image to the world people knew was "really" outside. This showed Stratton what a powerful role the brain plays in helping us see and how flexible it is in adapting to new situations. To prove the point further, when the people stopped wearing the glasses, they saw the world upside down once again, at least until their brains had made yet another readjustment.

We often say, "seeing is believing." But it is equally true that "appearances are deceiving." In fact, it sometimes turns out that "believing is seeing": People see what they believe to be true rather than what's actually out there.

For example, you know that the earth travels in orbit around the sun, yet you probably "see" the sun "rise" over the horizon every morning. For thousands of years humans had believed that their world was at center of things, in stationary orbit, circled by the sun. It took powerful arguments from the astronomer Copernicus to convince them that what they *seemed* to see was not correct. I'll discuss in Chapter 6 how this discovery helped to launch modern science.

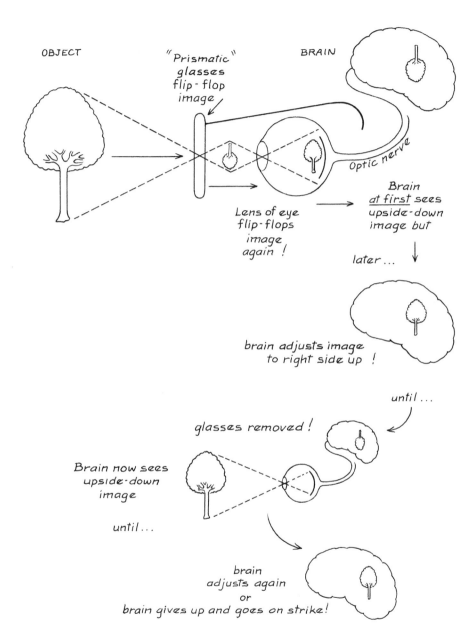

G. M. Stratton's Experiment

Another example: You've been told that the earth is round, and you've probably seen photographs of the "big blue marble" taken from outer space that show that it is a globe. But to tell the truth, doesn't the earth *look* flat to you? Or perhaps hilly and valleyish, but certainly not *round*. Little wonder the crew on Christopher Columbus's ship was frightened and angry when their skipper told them he was going around the world. They believed their eyes, which told them that the earth was flat and that they would sail off the edge. (No wonder, too, that a modern-day poll of first graders revealed that, no matter what they had been told in school, a majority believed in a flat world.)

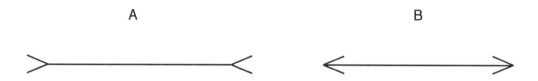

Here's another visual illusion. Perhaps you've seen it before. In fact, I *hope* you have seen it before, because that will prove another point about illusions. In the diagram, which of the lines is longer, A or B? The first-time viewer of the Muller-Lyer illusion generally thinks line A is longer. In fact, however, both lines are the same length. (Place a ruler on each of the lines if you're in doubt.) Because of the V-shaped lines at the ends, the eye—or the mind—is tricked into an error. But if you've seen this illusion before and know the answer, you weren't fooled. That is, like the people wearing glasses in Professor Stratton's experiment, you taught your mind to see what is "real." (But, as a smart person, you also need to be cautious; I could have tried to trick you as in the drawing on the next page!) You'll have to get your ruler to figure this one out. Which line is longest?

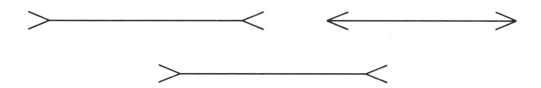

Does this seem a bit confusing? Complicated? Welcome to the amazing world of illusion and magic, where observing the unknown often turns out to be not what it seemed at all.

Illusions are not limited to the eye. Get an egg out of the fridge. Close your eyes. Cross your first two fingers; then gently stroke the egg. If you're like most people, you will feel *two* eggs. Because you are feeling a surface with the outer edges of those crossed fingers (rather than the inner edges, as is usual), your brain interprets the sensation as two separate objects. You can create the same illusion rubbing your nose, by the way, though it's harder to fool the brain, since it is very accustomed to thinking of you as having but one nose. It knows your nose, in short.

Taste is easily fooled too. As you know from science class, there are only four basic tastes—sweet, bitter, salt, and sour. But taste is more than tongue: It involves odors, sights, and textures as well. As a lad, I'm afraid I upset my grandmother when I used food coloring to dye some mashed potatoes dark blue. They tasted the same to me, but the blue spuds wrecked Granny's appetite. (A comedian, George Carlin, has remarked that in nature, "There's *no blue food!*")

Undaunted by the experience with my grandmother, I later angered some of my college friends by dyeing orange juice a dark and ugly green. It tasted the same, but people were upset by the color. Soft-drink manufacturers know that people expect certain tastes to be certain colors. They could produce orange soda pop, flavored by chemicals, that is crystal clear. Soda poppers actually inject orange coloring so it will look the way people expect "orange"-tasting products to look.

Here is yet another illustration: If you close your eyes, you may not be able to tell the difference between a raw potato and a raw carrot by taste. If you close your eyes and hold your nose, you may not even be able to distinguish an apple from an onion from a raw potato—they all crunch about the same. Seeing what you eat, or rather, *knowing* what you eat, has a lot to do with how your brain interprets what's coming in by way of the taste buds.

Your hearing can be tricked. Sometimes your brain hears things that aren't there or misinterprets sound waves. On a stormy night, the sound of a tree branch scraping the roof can become the clawing of a monster trying to get into the house. On a special winter's eve, a faint whistling of the wind can, to a child, sound very much like that of a red sleigh being towed by eight tiny reindeer.

As I was writing this section of the book, my wife called from another room to ask whether our neighbor's dog had gotten into the house again. We checked; no dog. We discovered that the clicking of the keys on my word processor had sounded like a dog's toenails clicking on the kitchen floor.

The philosopher Immanuel Kant once wrote, "Our senses do not deceive us. This is not because they always judge correctly, but because they do not judge at all." What Kant meant is that the *brain* does the judging and the interpreting. The senses merely supply raw information for the brain to fool around with.

Sometimes we see what people *expect* us to see. Do you remember the story "The Emperor's New Clothes"? The tailors (who were really *illusionists,* maybe even *hypnotists*) pretended to weave gorgeous clothes. Rather than look dumb, the emperor went along with it all, and so did his subjects. This led the emperor to appear stark raving naked in front of his people, who oohed and aahed as if he were wearing real clothes. It took a little girl, who refused to see what she was expected to see, to say, "But look: He's not wearing any clothes!"

Illusions go well beyond the five senses. Have you ever had a day when "time flew," when you got so absorbed in a project that time passed without your even knowing it? Or a time in school when things were so incredibly boring that time "stood still"? Of course the rate of time didn't change, but your perception of it certainly did.

The Long History of Illusion and Magic

In the previous chapters of this book, I've looked at myths, legends, folktales, superstitions, and supernatural creatures. Illusion and magic have links with each of these. As people have tried to understand the unknown, they've also been tricked by illusions, seeing what they wanted to see or what somebody else told them to see.

The Bible tells the story of the Hebrew prophet Aaron, who cast his staff on the ground and turned it into a serpent. Pharaoh called on his sorcerers to match the trick, which they did. However, Aaron's serpent ate up those of the temple wizards. How was it done? Some researchers speculate that Aaron and the priests might have learned

"Pot-Shots" by Ashleigh Brilliant. Copyright © 1985 by Ashleigh Brilliant. Reprinted by permission.

PROBING ON YOUR OWN

You are probably already master of some illusions, some tricks that were taught to you by friends or family. My dad taught me an illusion in which you pretend to bend a spoon by hiding the handle in your hands and letting the bowl of the spoon slide down the table. *(Kids: Don't try this trick unless you've been taught how it's done.)* And one of my friends in seventh grade showed me how to place a common pin in the inside angle of my elbow, then fold up my arm so it looks as if the pin is being driven right into the muscle. *(Kids: Don't do this.)* You may know how to fold your hands so it looks as if you have ten fingers, but only nine show. Or how to appear to rap your knuckles on the table with a fearsome noise (the noise made by a finger that you flip out as your hand descends). You've certainly tapped a friend on the far shoulder so he or she turns the wrong way, under the illusion that somebody's over there. You may know how to cast hand shadows that look like animals or people. Or how to knock on somebody's head so it sounds like wood. Maybe you know a few card tricks or other magical illusions. You may be good with puppets, so that people are engrossed and have a conversation with a figure of cloth. Now's the time to recollect those illusions. You might talk to friends and family to learn other tricks and illusions they know, such as pulling a coin out of somebody's ear. *(Kids: Don't put coins in your brothers' or sisters' ears.)*

how to hypnotize snakes so they would appear rigid, like walking sticks.

In ancient Greece, the temple priests were known to give soothsayers and oracles what seemed to be supernatural powers through the use of what we now call special effects. The priests designed huge temple doors, powered by hidden hydraulic systems, which would burst open although nobody was near them; they created candles or lamps, fueled by secret tanks, which would burn "forever"; they knew how to make "food for the gods" disappear overnight from locked rooms with secret entrances and passages.

Some of the most fascinating illusionists in history were the alchemists (*al*-kem-ists). From the beginning of recorded history, people have always been excited by the most valuable of metals: *gold*. Alchemists claimed to have the power to turn ordinary or "base" metals into gold.

There is some evidence that about three thousand years ago, Egyptian experimenters had figured out a simple process of electroplating, which is a way of using an electric current to "plate" or coat one metal with another. Archaeologists have discovered the remains of equipment that just might have worked to electroplate gold onto other metals. If so, Egyptian wizards could have created the illusion of alchemy by plating a thin film of gold onto objects. They weren't really creating gold, but to a believing and wishful audience, the trick would seem quite real.

Alchemy also excited the Greeks, who had a theory that the four basic elements were air, earth, water, and fire. They believed that everything on earth was made out of combinations of those ingredients and that elements could be changed from one form to another. You've watched liquid water turn into something hard—ice. You've seen flames "consume" wood and create smoke. You've seen dirt turn into mud and you've seen plants appear from plain dirt, as if by magic. It's not surprising, then, that the Greeks figured the idea of changing cheap and worthless stuff into gold was not only possible, but a terrific way to get rich.

Although there was no solid evidence that it actually worked, alchemy was practiced for over fifteen hundred years after the Egyptians and Greeks had experimented with it. Many alchemists spent much of their professional life looking for something called the "philosopher's stone," which would supposedly turn lead into gold.

Old prints depict alchemy

Although the alchemists failed in their quest, what they sought was not impossible. The "philosopher's stone" turns out to be a nuclear reactor! Modern-day scientists have found that under the proper conditions, it's possible to bombard a base metal, lead, with atomic particles and actually change it to gold. The trouble is, the process costs far more than it would take to buy gold in the first place, and the gold produced in a reactor is so radioactive that human beings could never go near it.

Illusionary Cures

Five hundred years ago—not long at all when you think of the millions of years this planet has existed—magic, science, myth, medicine, and illusion were all jumbled together. It was a time just before the "invention" of scientific thinking. In those pre-science days, many of the people experimenting with the unknown had several different occupations. Alchemists were also astrologers and fortune tellers. Some were physicians as well, using their understanding of nature to cure people. However, their medicine, like their alchemy, was rather a jumble of myth, legend, and superstition.

One of the leading alchemists, Paracelsus, claimed that he could cure sword wounds using the following "recipe." First, you had to obtain the sword that had done the damage (no easy task if it was the sword of an enemy who had just plunged it into your body!). Then you would start cooking! *(Kids: Don't brew this in your kitchen. Don't brew it anyplace!)*

> Take of moss growing on the head of a thief who has been hanged and left in the air; of real mummy; of human blood, still warm—of each one ounce; of human suet, two ounces; of linseed oil, turpentine, and Armenian bole—of each two drachms. Mix all well in a mortar, and keep the salve in an oblong, narrow urn.

The sword was then covered with this stuff; the wound was kept clean and covered with a bandage. By this process, Paracelsus claimed, the wound would heal. Modern doctors have pointed out that if you follow the same procedure of cleaning the wound, but leave out the part about the awful salve on the sword, people might get better on their own. It seems most unlikely that Paracelsus's goop was a part of the cure at all.

Animal Magnetism

The mix of medicine and magic also became tied up with magnetism. "Magical" rocks to which metal would cling had been known for thousands of years. Chinese experimenters understood enough about magnetism to create compasses five thousand years ago, and the Greeks and Egyptians also played around with magnetic objects.

As time passed, some alchemists came to believe that magnets might actually be a kind of philosopher's stone. A magnet magically draws pieces of metal to it with no human hand involved. Some alchemists and physicians began to experiment with magnets as a way of curing disease, figuring that a magnet might draw illness out of a body just as a magnet will draw iron filings to it.

The man who did most to promote this idea was one Franz Anton Mesmer, whose name, as you'll see, has been linked to a word we use commonly today. Mesmer was born in 1734 and, like many of the scientists of his time, wore several professional hats: He was an astronomer as well as an astrologer, but he had also studied medicine and practiced "astrological medicine"—trying to cure people by studying the supposed effects of the stars and planets on health.

Mesmer began experimenting with metal plates and magnets applied to the human body. His idea was to pretend that the magnets were stars and planets and to place them on the body in the same positions they occupied in the sky. With the supposed power of magnets to cure disease, what Mesmer saw as the natural action of the stars and planets would be speeded up.

Then Mesmer came to believe that the world was filled with an invisible "magnetic fluid" and that he could produce cures merely by waving his hands over the human body, shaping the flow of this magical fluid. Sometimes people under his influence would enter a trancelike state, hypnotized by the moving of hands. Anton Mesmer developed such a reputation that he was able to open a *salon* in Paris, France, where wealthy people came to be cured.

Mesmer's patients would enter his lavishly decorated rooms to find a tank filled with "magnetized water." Numerous pipes stuck out of the sides. People would apply the magical water to the parts of their body that were broken or diseased. Next Mesmer's assistants would enter the room and massage patients, getting them into a hypnotic trance. Finally, Anton Mesmer himself would arrive with a great flourish and pronounce people cured. And many patients agreed with him: "I am *cured!*"

What was happening? Modern analysts figure that Mesmer's effects had nothing to do with magnetism. His patients would be lulled into a quiet state and then drift into a trance. Because they believed in Mesmer and his animal magnetism, they *believed* themselves to be cured. They had been "mesmerized," a term we use today to describe a person who has been totally absorbed or captivated.

At the time, there was a great deal of suspicion about Mesmer and his cures. Many thought he was a quack, a fake. Therefore the French government gathered experts to examine his work. This group, including American Benjamin Franklin, looked closely at Mesmer's work and concluded that there was no science behind it. Mesmer was exposed as a fraud and forced to leave Paris, although he took a considerable fortune with him.

Looking back at the whole thing, we realize that Mesmer, in his way, may have been on to something. We know that some diseases exist more in the mind than in the body, and hypnosis is used by modern doctors as a cure. So some of Mesmer's patients probably did get better as a result of his work. Nevertheless, his work was so jumbled up with superstition and false science that he was quite properly put out of business. Perhaps most important is to realize that Mesmer was successful only because of *illusions,* ideas that existed in the minds of his patients. It's also important to note that we are talking about medical fakery that took place as little as two hundred years ago!

Fakes in Scholarship

We think of "scholarship" as a quest for truth and understanding in probing the unknown. But scholars, too, can fall prey to illusions and sometimes have even been guilty of creating deceptions or downright fakes. One of the most famous cases of fakery took place not five hundred or two hundred years ago, but in this century. It's the story of "Piltdown Man," and it happened in 1912.

In that year, Arthur Smith Woodward of the British Museum was presented with a human skull by a geologist, Charles Dawson, who explained that he had found it among archaeological diggings near Piltdown, England. As Woodward and Dawson studied the skull, they discovered that although its cranium (or brain case) was like that of a man, its jaw was apelike. After careful research, they concluded they had discovered the "missing link," an ancient creature that was believed to connect modern humans with apes. They named it *Eoanthropus dawsoni,* "Dawson's Dawn Man."

Although a few people voiced doubts, most scholars accepted the findings of Dawson and Woodward. However, later analysis revealed that the jaw was that of a modern-day monkey, stained to make it look half a million years old. The top part—the cranium—was authentically old. The two had been placed together as a hoax. Nobody to this day knows for sure who created this fake. One theory says that Charles Dawson himself both created and "discovered" the skull, perhaps thinking it would bring him fame (which it did). Another explanation is that an assistant to Dawson created the skull as a joke, then was afraid to explain the gag after everybody took it seriously. In any case, researchers have noted that Arthur Smith Woodward, the British Museum curator, had the scholarly knowledge necessary to figure out the fake. He *should* have spotted the fraud, but failed to. Why? This turns out to be another case of "believing is seeing." Many scholars think Woodward fell for the illusion because he *wanted* to believe that this skull was the "missing link." He saw with his heart rather than his mind.

Other faked discoveries have succeeded because researchers *wanted* to see a particular result. In one case, an archaeologist found a set of animal bones in a pit. He reassembled them, fitting all the bones together, and discovered a *unicorn,* the mythical beast with one horn in the center of its forehead. Later examination showed that the bones could be reassembled in a different way and were the skeleton of an ordinary horse. The researcher had been led astray by his wishful thinking.

Mistaking evidence for what one wants to see is not limited to days gone by. James Randi is a modern-day magician who specializes in studying hoaxes and frauds. He is especially critical of the work of a Swiss investigator, Erich von Daniken, whose book *Chariots of the Gods?* claims that the earth has been visited by creatures from outer space. Von Daniken presents as evidence the pyramids of Egypt, as well as long lines scratched in the earth in Peru. James Randi has looked at the evidence and finds Von Daniken guilty of the same wishful thinking that led to misunderstandings of Piltdown Man and the "unicorn" skeleton.

PROBING ON YOUR OWN

Many interesting books have been written about errors and hoaxes. There's the tale of the *archeopterix*, which was first said to be a "missing link" type bird. It turned out to be a faked "flying lizard" with "fossil" wings made from contemporary chicken feathers. There's the story of N-rays, which were reported by a French researcher earlier in this century, but turned out to be mostly wishful thinking. And, of course, there is the whole wonderful debate over UFOs—unidentified flying objects—and whether they are real or merely the fanciful illusion of people who want to believe that extraterrestrials have come to earth in superfast space vehicles. To investigate these stories further, see the references for this chapter or check at your local library under some of the following headings: Science and Pseudoscience; Hoax; Fraud.

Illusion and Entertainment

Not all illusions are evil or intended to mislead people or give them false impressions about the world they live in. For hundreds of years, illusions have been a part of entertainment, a harmless way for people to have fun. In fact, most of us rather enjoy being tricked—even "mesmerized"—by amazing performances.

About the same time that Anton Mesmer was mesmerizing his clients, jugglers walked the streets of the great cities. They were the illusionists and magicians of their time. Of course, juggling itself is a kind of illusion, seeming to defy gravity as a juggler keeps three, four, or five objects in the air at the same time. But jugglers had many tricks in their bag, as shown in this poem by John Gay:

> A Juggler long through all the town
> Had raised his fortune and renown.
> You'd think (so far his art transcends)
> The devil at his finger tips.

This juggler played the old cups and balls trick (one ball is placed under one of three cups and the passersby try to guess which one it's under). He had a deck of cards that was "obedient to his words." He could draw ivory eggs out of chickens; he was able to make bank notes disappear. (His assistants could make bank notes disappear, too, and John Gay warned people not to become so absorbed in the magic show that pickpockets could empty their wallets undetected.)

The theater has always been a great source of illusion. When you go to a play, you are a part of an imaginary world from the very beginning. Stage sets and props are carefully designed to look realistic to the audience, and special effects are used to create sounds and sights from real life.

One of the most famous theatrical illusions of a century ago was "Pepper's ghost," created by Professor John Pepper. Ghosts appear in many plays, and producers want to create an illusion of the spirit world. Now in staging a play with a ghost, you could dress a performer in a ghostly costume and have him or her just walk onstage. However, audiences demand something more, a greater illusion.

Professor Pepper, who was actually a science teacher, understood the laws of optics, how light travels and is reflected or bent by glass. He would place a pane of glass in front of the stage, then skillfully arrange mirrors and a lantern beneath the stage to cast an image on the glass. At the appropriate moment in the play, he would turn on the lantern, and a costumed actor beneath the stage would have his ghostly image reflected off the pane of glass, even as the audience could look through the glass to see the stage as usual. Pepper's ghost seemed to come from nowhere and dazzled London audiences. However, after a while, people figured out the illusion, and it is said that young boys in the audience would spoil the effect by throwing wads of paper and bouncing them off the glass, exposing the trick.

Another popular ghost illusion used a cloud of smoke and a projection lamp to create a wavery image, very ghostlike, very convincing, that would simply vanish into thin air.

Of course, these illusions of one hundred years ago would not fool us today. Illusionists must learn to stay one step ahead of the audience. What seems magical today may seem very ordinary tomorrow.

Magic Tricks

In a way, magic goes a step beyond probing the unknown into *controlling* the unknown. The magician is like the prophet or the witch doctor or the alchemist in that he or she seems to have powers over forces that the rest of us do not understand. Of course, this control is an illusion. The magician has merely figured out how to use the known to give the impression he or she is in charge of the unknown.

Many illusions that were invented centuries ago still seem pretty amazing to us today. When you see a magician make somebody disappear or saw a person in half or make a person rise in the air without any visible support, you are often seeing tricks that have been part of magicians' bags of tricks for generations. Illusionists become very skilled at their craft, and their tricks are carefully planned and staged. One famous magician, Robert Houdin, practiced doing many things at once, for example, juggling while reading a book. Thus he could, for instance, show the audience an empty box even while slipping something into that box. Robert Houdin so impressed another illusionist that the great Houdini borrowed his last name.

Many illusions are extraordinarily complicated and well prepared.

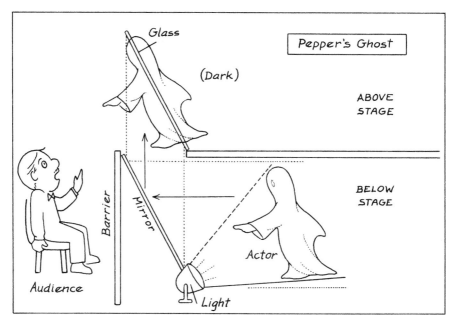

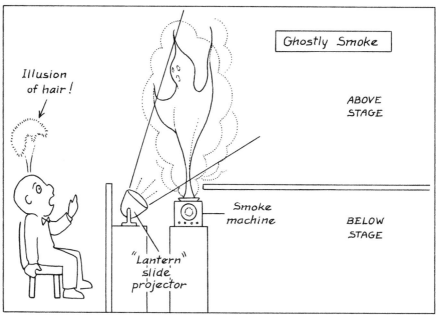

Ghost Illusions

The magician shows you a lady lying on a board that is supported by chairs. As he talks to you, an assistant slips a metal bar into the back of the board and "levitates" the person. The magician talks up a storm to the audience, showing that there are no supports, but he has skillfully planned his demonstration so that he never steps across the supporting bar.

Or a person steps inside a closet and disappears. The trick? Mirrors fold out from the inside walls, giving the appearance of an empty box and leading to the expression "It's done with mirrors."

Some tricks involve several people wearing identical costumes so that a person can disappear from the stage and reappear elsewhere in the room. There are head-chopping-off tricks with fake heads; tricks that involve trapdoors and hidden assistants (sometimes small children squeezed into small spaces); tricks with special knots that look real but slip apart when the magician is locked into a box.

Not all magical illusions are really tricks. For example, some sword swallowers actually swallow swords, having trained for years to be able to slide a straight sharp object from mouth to stomach. *(Kids: Guess what not even to think about doing!)* Fire eaters actually pop burning fluids into their mouths. More often, however, illusions are involved. For example, some sword swallowers fake it with swords that collapse into their own handles to create a trick. Eating fire is sometimes done trickily by snuffing the flame before it enters the mouth. Or a fire eater may spit a flammable liquid from his or her mouth so that it catches fire only after it leaves the lips. *(Kids: Don't you try fire tricks under any circumstances.)*

Pictures that Move

In our day, stage magicians and illusionists are not as popular as they once were. They have been overshadowed by one of the most persuasive illusions of all: the moving picture. Through film and television, people have seen the impossible—mice and ducks that talk; creatures from other planets; heroes who overcome incredible odds

PROBING ON YOUR OWN

It's said that a magician will never tell you his or her secrets, but if you're willing to do a little research, you can master many illusions yourself. You can go to a magic shop—there's probably one in your city or town—and purchase magic tricks, complete with explanations. More interesting and challenging is to check out some books from the library and to make your own props, gadgets, and illusions. With practice—and it takes a lot—you could become a magician and illusionist. There's even money to be made entertaining at parties as a young professional magician, and that's no illusion.

and dangers; heroines who are not only glamorous, but fly. We've seen people die and come to life again; we've watched "extinct" dinosaurs that seem absolutely real; we have witnessed the lives of people who died long before our time. All this has been done through the magic of the moving picture.

TV and movies are a form of visual illusion. What we see are not moving objects or people, but a series of "still" pictures flashed before our eyes at high speed. Just as the brain filled in gray spots in the Hermann Grid illusion, it fills in the gaps between still pictures and gives us the impression of motion. As filmmakers have developed more and more sophisticated technology, they have been able to create more and more realistic illusions.

Thirty or forty years ago, movies about outer space—movies like the original Buck Rogers serials—featured rockets which, to today's eyes, clearly resemble tin cans taped together. We're used to the very fancy special effects of the latest Star Trek films and television programs, with visual illusions that make it seem as if we're deep in outer space.

Even beyond the special effects, TV and film have the ability to make the characters played by actors and actresses come to life.

When you see a drama at the theater, you're often aware that this is "just a play," whereas moving pictures have a way of entrancing, of "mesmerizing" you. Some adults are concerned that young people sometimes confuse the vividness of TV and film for the real world, that they try to transfer the fantasy of the screen world to their own lives.

In this book I can't begin to scratch the surface of the magical world of moving pictures. There are many long and detailed histories about TV and film and numerous books on the technology that is used to create the illusions of "TV magic" or "film wizardry." Check your library for a book on the history of moving pictures.

From Illusion to Reality

There's an interesting story about Peter Tapatai, a Canadian Inuit Indian who has his own television show, a show that is broadcast in the Inuktitut language to serve the Indian population. At one point in preparing a show, Peter and his producer decided to have Peter poke fun at superheroes like Superman. Peter put on long red underwear, a blue cape, and rubber boots. He became "Super Shamou," representing a mythical shaman, a legendary Inuit character.

Using simple visual television tricks, technicians superimposed Peter's body on another picture so that he appeared to fly. Few people were fooled by the illusion; it was, after all, a gag. In fact, the producer insisted that Peter appear on the show in ordinary settings, just so children wouldn't think he could actually fly. But a funny thing happened. Peter Tapatai has become a kind of superhero in his own right. People enjoyed seeing Super Shamou, and they liked the kind of advice Peter was giving kids about staying in school, not getting involved with drugs, and taking pride in who you are and what you are. Peter now travels across Canada in his homemade superhero outfit, telling young people about Inuit traditions. He began his television career with illusion and became "real" in the process, an example of illusion and magic at its best.

The Crystal Ball of Magic and Illusion

It's interesting to speculate about the future of magic and illusion. You'd think that as the world grows older, as we learn more and more about the unknown, magic and illusion would become less important. But it seems that people do not lose their interest in illusions. People *like* to be fooled, provided it's not for evil purposes. Technological advances promise to make even today's illusions look ordinary. When holographs—three-dimensional laser photographs— are perfected to appear real as life, someone may make a holograph of Professor Pepper's ghost, and that ghost, real as life, will walk up and say to you, "Tell me, what's been going on in the two centuries since I died?"

PROBING ON YOUR OWN

It's possible for you to experiment with the optical illusions of films and television.

Make a "flip movie." On a series of index cards, draw nearly identical stick figures, each drawing showing a slightly different position, moving a hand or foot slightly. When you flip through the drawings, you get the illusion of motion. Can you create a figure that appears to walk or wave or throw a baseball?

Look for a book on special-effects photography. With many "household" cameras you can do trick photos, such as showing yourself shaking hands with yourself or having your face appear twice in a family portrait.

Some home movie cameras have a feature that lets you take one frame of film at a time. With such a camera you can make your own animated cartoons.

Use a home video camera to create an adventure show set in some exotic location: the jungle, outer space, inside a giant's belly button. What tricks can you play to make your setting look real to the viewer?

5

Reason and Logic

In other chapters, I have mentioned Sherlock Holmes, the fictional detective who is occasionally puzzled, but never fooled, who solves cases by sheer brainpower, dazzling the world (and especially the police) with his analytic powers.

Holmes's powers were demonstrated in the very first story in the series, the novel *A Study in Scarlet,* written in 1887. Immediately after being introduced to Dr. Watson, he remarks: "You have been in Afghanistan, I perceive."

Watson is naturally astonished. How could someone know that much about him without advance information? Holmes explains:

> I *knew* you came from Afghanistan. From long habit the train of thoughts ran so swiftly through my mind that I arrived at the conclusion without being conscious of the intermediate steps. There were such steps, however. The train of reasoning ran, "Here is a gentleman of a medical type, but with the air of a military man. Clearly an army doctor, then. He has just come from the tropics, for his face is dark, and that is not the natural tint of his skin, for his wrists are fair. He has undergone hardship and sickness, as his haggard face says clearly. His left arm has been injured. He holds it in a stiff and unnatural manner.

Where in the tropics could an English army doctor have seen such hardship and got his arm wounded? Clearly in Afghanistan."

Says Watson, "It is simple enough as you explain it."

Of course it was not so simple. Sherlock Holmes had spent years practicing his powers of observation and reason in order to perform such a feat with brainpower. Part of the fun of the Sherlock Holmes stories is watching Holmes's mind at work, comparing his explanation to your own and to those proposed by his faithful sidekick, Watson.

Sherlock Holmes is only one of many, many logical detectives in fiction and on film and TV. Another famous sleuth is Inspector Hercule Poirot, a creation of novelist Agatha Christie. Poirot uses the "little gray cells" of his brain to solve crimes. Christie likes to bring all the suspects into a room in the final chapter of the book and to have Poirot carefully reveal his thinking about the crime and identify the guilty person. Or person*s*: In one famous Hercule Poirot story, *Murder on the Orient Express,* it turns out that *everybody* committed the crime. The clever Poirot figures out that since everybody on the train seems to have an alibi, the crime must have been committed by everybody on the train, working together!

PROBING ON YOUR OWN

Fictional detectives like Holmes and Poirot have been used as models for TV detectives. Think of programs that have a man or woman who sifts through small clues and details to come up with clever explanations of a crime, who captures a criminal who had planned the "perfect crime." You'll also find satires of those kinds of heroes, detectives who are comic bunglers. Next time you watch one of those shows, keep a notepad in hand and write down what seem to be the clues to the crime. Can you solve the mystery before the TV program tells you whodunit?

Now, in real life there *are* intelligent people who can think powerfully and imaginatively to explain the peculiar or the puzzling. As a matter of fact, you undoubtedly have such powers yourself. You may not use them to solve crimes and, if you're like many people, you may not exercise those skills as much as you could or should. But the little gray cells stuffed inside your skull can solve all kinds of mysteries.

Philip and Phyllis Morrison have observed, "Written everywhere in the landscapes of the world and under its oceans are . . . subtle clues." The skillful observer and thinker "can read there natural dramas in many acts." Their book, *The Ring of Truth,* shows how men and women have become more and more skillful about reading such clues so that we now know a surprising amount about the origins of the universe, even though none of us was around at the beginning of time to write down the story or take pictures. The same kinds of clues to the dramas of the universe can be found in the stars; in the weather; in trees, birds, and fish; even in human tools and machines—from the cave dweller's ax to a high-powered automobile sitting in the street outside your home. Sherlock Holmes phrased this idea well when he said that just by studying a drop of water and thinking carefully about it, a person could predict "the possibility of an Atlantic or a Niagara without having seen or heard of one or the other."

In earlier chapters of this book we've seen what happens when people accept myth, magic, or illusion as an explanation of what's going on around them. Although it may be tempting to suppose that great mountains were created by even greater giants or that the oceans came about from the tears of mermaids, inquiring minds want to find a more satisfying truth. As the world has advanced, we've developed a greater understanding about one gadget or tool that helps us figure out truth and separate it from myth or falsehood. That gizmo is the human brain.

A Thinking Machine

Although science knows a great deal about the brain's workings, it remains an extraordinary mystery. By rough estimate, the human brain contains about 100 billion nerve cells, a number so large we can hardly imagine it. We know that it uses electrical impulses and generates chemicals to send messages. We understand that certain thinking and memory processes are stored in certain parts of the brain, and we have found that the brain's processes can be altered through the use of alcohol, drugs, or even suggestions from a hypnotist.

As scientists, philosophers, doctors, and teachers have attempted to understand the brain, they have developed many models or illustrations to help them describe their view more easily. For example, people have compared the functioning of the brain to a telephone network, with "lines" stretching out to every part of the body. You can then "phone" any part of your body, send it a message, and get it to do what you want. That's not a bad comparison, but it falls short of describing *all* the brain's powers. It doesn't explain reflex actions—such as when you instinctively jump away from something dangerous without thinking about it. For a telephone to work this way, you'd have to have a phone that *anticipated* an incoming call and was answered before the phone rang.

As we saw in the last chapter, the eye-brain connection has been compared to a camera, but you know that the brain offers its own explanation of the pictures it takes. Brains have been compared to calculators (crunching data at a great rate), to muscles (that require exercise to stay in shape), to devils and angels (representing our good and bad sides), even to grinding machines (breaking information into small pieces). But no single model of the brain seems to capture all of the mind's wonderful powers.

About one hundred fifty years ago, a pseudoscience called phrenology was fashionable. Phrenologists claimed to be able to map the brain and to judge how smart a person was by studying the shape of his or her head. We now know that particular functions are located in

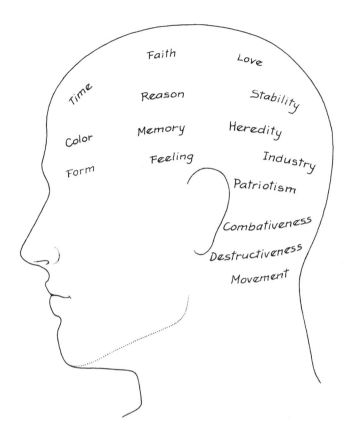

Phrenologist's Map of the Mind

particular areas of the brain, but there's no real connection between the brain's shape and size and its functioning. So the search for an explanation of the brain goes on.

For a long, long time, people have found the idea of a "mechanical" mind attractive. Wouldn't it be terrific if our machinelike brains just took over and solved life's mysteries for us? The modern version of the brain as machine idea is the brain as computer. In "Star Trek," for example, the starship *Enterprise* is mostly run by a computer, one that talks, gives advice, and from time to time takes over the ship and runs it by itself. In many other science-fiction stories, films, and TV shows you'll see computers, robots, and "smart" people that "think" without imperfections. It's as if we long for a machinelike brain, an answer-giving machine that doesn't have human "faults," such as feelings, to get in the way.

But we are not computers or thinking machines. Our feelings and emotions sometimes do get in the way, causing us to come up with answers that a computer would zap as illogical. The brain sometimes makes errors or comes up with false explanations as we probe the unknown. At the same time, the fact that our brain is a human organ, not a computer, lets it and us do some pretty amazing things that are far beyond the reach of the ordinary, emotion-free computer. On "Star Trek," it's almost always the humans who, in the end, figure out what's best to do.

PROBING ON YOUR OWN

You might enjoy drawing a "map" or representation of your own brain, trying to show how yours seems to work best. Are you basically an orderly or organized thinker? If so, you might draw the innards of your mind as gears and wheels. Maybe you're wild and fanciful as a thinker, mulling over all kinds of stuff in a dizzying array. If so, you could sketch your mind as a series of squiggles. If you're a dreamer, figure out a way to show your visions. You can also represent your brain by some of its/your interests, say, your hobbies or some of the things you like to do in your free time. Use symbols—a bike, a postage stamp, a book—to show how you think. Include sports, music, art, TV, drama, and so on. Your brain map might show your funny side as well as your serious side, your ability to feel empathy with other people as well as your need to take care of your own interests. You can keep your brain map private or show it to your parents and friends and discuss how you think.

How Thinking Goes Astray

Jessica Davidson says that the search for understanding *isn't* like an Easter egg hunt, where you go out and suddenly find the "truth" in a colorful package just waiting for you to pick it up. She adds that knowledge is not like a brick, either, something that you can just pick up and carry around or build walls with.

A better example (though not exact) is that knowledge is a little like a bowl of Jell-O, squishy, shaky, filled with tremors and trembling, not easy to pick up with a spoon or with your fingers. Of course, there are some facts that we can know and use with confidence: 2 + 2 = 4; things fall down, not up. But wait. Even "up" and "down" aren't always that clear. As a child, you probably were amazed to learn that on the far side of the globe, at this very moment, people think they are standing up, but they are pointed 180 degrees away from us. What is "up" in a seemingly endless universe? What's "up" in a spaceship where the occupants are weightless? What's up, doc?

Even more complicated are ideas like "right," "wrong," and the "truth." Like "up" and "down," such ideas often "just depend" on where you are standing at the moment or on what you think is important. Because our brains are not like computers, we don't always find truth lying in the grass like a brightly colored Easter egg. We seldom find it printed out in nice clear letters by our computer.

As amazing as our senses and brains are, they are also limited, both in what they can do and in the information they receive. Our eyes can detect only a part of the electromagnetic waves called light. We can't see the infrared and ultraviolet varieties, for example. That means we just can't see big chunks of our world. In fact, some good science-fiction stories have been written about human beings who could see these hidden dimensions, whose "sensors" could pick up TV and radio signals. (You also know from Chapter 2 that some people think they have special powers to "see" the spirit world of ghosts and ghoulies.) Sometimes our senses depend on what's around them. What we call "hot" or "cold" is determined by our own skin, and you know yourself that what passes for a warm day in winter would seem like a real chiller in the summertime.

John Godfrey Saxe describes the unreliability of the senses in a poem called "The Blind Men and the Elephant." Six blind men were asked to feel an elephant and describe it. One man touched the side of the beast and declared the elephant to be like a wall. A second touched the tusk and said the elephant was like a spear. The man touching the trunk called it a snake, whereas the man touching a knee said it was rather like a tree. The ear toucher said the elephant was like a fan, whereas the tail toucher insisted it was like a rope. "And so these men," concluded Saxe,

> Disputed loud and long,
> Each in his own opinion,
> Exceeding stiff and strong.
> Though each was partly in the right,
> And all were in the wrong.

In short, we must be very careful about what we declare to be the "truth" on the basis of what our senses and our brains tell us.

Nevertheless, in spite of these limitations, our brain does something as regular as clockwork: *It makes patterns.* From the time you were born (and very likely before you were born), your brain was processing information and looking for things that happen the same way. When our brain detects a pattern, this helps us make sense out of what's going on around us. We use patterns to help us figure something out the next time.

For example, babies quickly learn that human faces mean help is on the way; they learn where their next meal is coming from; they learn that crying is a way to get somebody to do something about whatever is ailing them at the moment.

The brain detects patterns in sound, and pretty soon it teaches you to use a language or to hum a tune. It sees patterns in color and shape, and eventually you can take a pencil and draw pictures that resemble what you see in the world. The brain sees patterns in events and teaches you to duck when a bee flies your way, and it can calculate the flight pattern of a snowball or rotten tomato to hit a moving target such as your worst enemy.

Even when you're not aware of it, your brain is sifting and sorting through sights, sounds, words, feelings, putting them into patterns so that next time you will recognize things a little bit quicker.

Edward DeBono has observed that this pattern-making capability of the brain "allows us to make sense of the world and to live. Without such a system, life would be impossible." At the same time, he warns, the brain is, in its way, "brilliantly uncreative," because once it has identified a pattern, it often keeps using that same pattern, *even if that pattern is not 100 percent correct.*

Mark Twain, the author of *Tom Sawyer,* once said that a cat that sat on a hot stove wouldn't sit on a hot stove again, but it wouldn't sit on a cold one, either. The cat forms a pattern (or simply "has an idea"): "If you sit on the stove, you get your fanny burned." But because the cat is not as good a thinker as a human being, it doesn't realize that the problem is *heat,* not just the stove. Therefore it wrongly avoids all stoves, rather than just hot ones.

People can make more sophisticated patterns than cats can, but we, too, have our weaknesses. Sometimes we stay with a pattern just because it has been around a long time. We may use a pattern, not because we thought of it ourselves, but because somebody told us it was true. We don't always think very carefully about our impressions, and we just jump to wrong conclusions. As wonderful as the brain is, it's sometimes quite lazy or supercautious in moving into new or unexplored territory.

That helps to explain some of the things we've looked at in the preceding chapters: myths, illusions, magic, folkways. If an explanation seems to work, if a pattern seems to explain the unknown, we often hang on to it. Thus it was very difficult for Columbus to persuade people that the earth was round. A pattern was set in people's minds; the eyes "seemed" to show a flat earth; and people called Columbus a crazy man, even though he was right.

If you don't understand something that's going on and a magician performs a trick or an illusion, you may believe he or she has found an Easter egg of truth. Further, if you think you've found an Easter egg of truth and somebody comes along to tell you it's a rotten egg, you may not be ready to receive the news. History is filled with stories of people who had correct new ideas but were punished or even killed because other people wanted to cling to an old idea, an old explanation, a familiar pattern.

The powers of the brain give us knowledge, learning, and understanding, even as those powers also give us superstition, myth, fear, and even bigotry and hatred. Thus we human beings find ourselves in what logicians call a dilemma, a situation where we don't really know whether to trust the brain fully or not. Is seeing believing? Does thinking provide right answers or merely lead to ignorance and superstition?

One of the ways out of the dilemma is to exercise a power that seems to be unique to human beings. We can actually *think about our own thinking,* and thus we can think about whether or not we are thinking rightly or wrongly. Thinking about thinking can be somewhat dizzying. It's a little like holding up a mirror to a mirror.

PROBING ON YOUR OWN

Find a small hand mirror and stand in front of a bathroom mirror. Now place the small mirror on your forehead—shiny side out. The small mirror will reflect what's in the large mirror and vice versa. As you manipulate the small mirror slightly, you will see a series of images: you holding a mirror that shows you holding a mirror that shows you holding a mirror and so on, theoretically forever and ever. You'll observe, too, that the images seem to form a tunnel that bores right through your head, going deeper and deeper. That endless tunnel into your mind is sort of what thinking about thinking is all about.

Entering Logic Land

The tunnel of the mind is the land of logic and reason. You've heard of logic or logical thinking many times in your life. "Be logical." "That doesn't seem logical to me." Your commonsense definition of logic is probably something like "things that make sense."

Technically, logic is the art and science of knowing whether or not arguments are valid. Another way of putting it is to say that logic studies the patterns of thinking to determine whether or not conclusions make sense.

Example: An acorn fell on Chicken Little's head. "The sky is falling," she concluded, and she threw the entire barnyard into a great uproar. Chicken Little's sister, Chicken Logician (sounds almost like a fast-food chain, doesn't it?), would step back and analyze:

"Hmm. You say the sky is falling. What evidence do you have? Are there pieces of blue sky lying about? Has this ever happened before? How did you conclude that the sky is tumbling about your feathery head?"

In the children's story, Chicken Little eventually figures out that the sky is *not* falling, but it takes her a long time. Chicken Logician says we don't have to run about, wildly flapping our wings. We can put the little gray cells to work, analyzing our past experiences, thinking about what we know, and determining what makes sense.

The study of logic can be traced back to the Greeks, with whom so much of our knowledge as well as our mythology begins. About 2300 years ago Greek philosophers developed a model or pattern for thinking called the syllogism. It had three parts: It began with two premises (statements that you believe to be true), then drove to a conclusion. Here is one of the most famous of the Greek syllogisms:

PREMISE 1: All men are mortal.
PREMISE 2: Socrates is a man.
CONCLUSION: Socrates is mortal.

Now, that may not seem like a very spectacular conclusion. We pretty much knew that Socrates was mortal from looking at him. Nevertheless, the syllogism allowed the Greeks to speculate about how we reach conclusions. Further, there is much fun to be had playing around with *false* syllogisms—arguments that seem to fit the pattern but are neither true nor valid. For example:

PREMISE 1: All dogs have fleas.
PREMISE 2: There's a flea on my arm!
CONCLUSION: I am a dog.

Why isn't this "logical"? The Greeks figured out that your first and second premises had to have at least one part in common, one word (such as *fleas* or *dogs*) that links the premises. In the example above, it was illogical to conclude that having a flea on a human arm meant that the person was a hound.

Suppose we changed PREMISE 2: "There's a flea on Fido." Could we conclude that "Fido is a dog"? At first you might think so. But under logic (and common sense), you recognize that merely having a flea wouldn't make something a dog. Fido could, in fact, be a chicken! A chicken with fleas. One correct syllogism on this topic would read:

PREMISE 1: All dogs have fleas.
PREMISE 2: Fido is a dog.
CONCLUSION: Fido has fleas.

But common sense finds another problem here. Not *all* dogs have fleas. As the Greeks discovered, you can have perfectly logical arguments, but if your premises are incorrect, you will come up with correct but untrue answers. Probably the most accurate logical syllogism we could put together on this topic is this:

PREMISE 1: Some dogs have fleas.
PREMISE 2: Fido is a dog.
CONCLUSION: Fido *may* have fleas (but then again, Fido may *not*).

Logic, then, doesn't automatically supply one with truth. There's a modern saying about computers: "Garbage in; garbage out." The same is true of syllogisms! If you form a faulty syllogism, you'll come up with wrong answers even if you follow the right patterns:

> PREMISE 1: Something fell on my head.
> PREMISE 2: Looking up, I see the sky.
> CONCLUSION: The sky is falling!

"Garbage!" says Chicken Logician, who might reason:

> PREMISE 1: Something fell on my head.
> PREMISE 2: I don't see anything above except blue sky.
> CONCLUSION: I think I'll look around on the ground to see if I can figure out what bonked me. Ah, there's an acorn!

Sherlock Holmes regarded logic as a *tool* for understanding. He said,

> I consider that a man's brain originally is like a little empty attic, and you have to stock it with such furniture as you can. A fool takes all the lumber of every sort that he comes across, so that the knowledge which might be useful to him gets crowded out. . . . Now the skillful workman is very careful as to what he takes into his brain-attic. He will have nothing but the tools which may help him in doing his work. . . .

Holmes favored mastering the skills of thinking rather than simply piling up knowledge for its own sake. So does Chicken Logician.

The Snake that Bites Itself: Paradoxes

While playing around with logic, the Greek philosophers also discovered some logical *paradoxes,* which are statements that seem logical but prove false or lead to nonsensical conclusions. They would represent a paradox with a drawing of a snake eating its own tail— feeding on itself. Chicken Logician's favorite paradox is "Which came first, the chicken or the egg?" If you argue that the chicken came first and gave forth an egg, somebody can point out that chickens come from eggs. But if you say the egg was first, the arguer

PROBING ON YOUR OWN

You might enjoy reading some more about logic. An especially good book is Jessica Davidson's *The Square Root of Tuesday* (see the references for this chapter). She shows several ways to map logical arguments, including the use of circle diagrams to show logic at work.

Some dogs have fleas.
Fido is a dog.
Does Fido have fleas?

All dogs are mammals.
Fido is a dog.
Fido is a mammal.

Where would you "logically" put Fido?

If you can't find Jessica Davidson's book, look in the card catalog under "Logic" for a beginner's book on logic.

can observe that it must have come from an existing chicken. It's a snake feeding on itself—a chicken hatching itself!—a paradox.

Here's a paradox created by Zeno of Elia over two thousand years ago: You can logically prove to a friend that he or she cannot possibly get from this side of the room to the other side. Here's how Zeno's Paradox works:

YOU: Would you agree with me that before you can cross the room, you have to go halfway?

FRIEND: Sure.

YOU :   But before you can go halfway across the room, you have to go halfway of that half?

FRIEND: Uh, yes.

YOU: And before you can cross half of the half, you have to cross half of that?

FRIEND: Why yes, oh wise person.

YOU: (*Triumphantly*) Well, you see this could go on forever. You can't cross the room because you can't even cross halfway!

FRIEND: Amazing. And it used to seem so easy!

Zeno had a number of paradoxes. He could prove that an arrow in flight was standing still. He could prove that a rabbit could never catch up to a tortoise that had had a head start. (Before the rabbit can pass the tortoise, it must catch up to where the tortoise was; but by the time the rabbit gets to where it was, the tortoise has moved on.)

These are logic games. Although your friend may accept your argument about crossing a room halfway, he or she *can still cross the room.* The hare *can* catch up to the tortoise, and will. The way out of a paradox is to pull the tail out of the snake's mouth, to step outside the logical argument. For instance, the way out of the room-crossing paradox is to observe that just because you go halfway before you go all the way, you don't have to *stop* in the middle. And that rabbit *can* pass the tortoise because it doesn't stop at the point where the tortoise was, but will zoom past, leaving the turtle eating the dust of logic.

Chicken Logician will break the chicken-egg paradox by telling you that its ancestors evolved from lower and lower beasts. What came first turns out to be amino acids in a great ocean, even before there was any life on this planet.

PROBING ON YOUR OWN

Still More Paradoxes

Can you figure out ways to break each of the following paradoxes?

This sentence has six words.

This sentence is a lie.

Never say never.

Only a fool would read this sentence.

There is nothing so unthinkable about thought unless it be the absence of thought.   SAMUEL BUTLER

Practical Logic for Common and Uncommon Mysteries

Obviously logic isn't much good unless it helps you solve problems in everyday life or come up with explanations of things you don't originally understand. Since the days of the Greek syllogism, thinkers have realized that there's such a thing as practical logic, something that says, "If you're worried that your dog has fleas, check out its skin or, to be safe, dust it with flea powder." To do either one or both would be quite logical, even though you didn't run the idea through a syllogism.

Because of the complicated nature of the brain, reaching logical conclusions is equally complicated. What you decide to do about your dog is based on:

PROBING ON YOUR OWN

Another interesting example of a paradox is something called the Moebius strip. Take a strip of paper as shown. Give it a half twist and glue or tape the ends together. You'll come up with a loop. With a pencil, draw a line down the middle of one side of the loop—keep going. If you go all the way around, you'll come back to where you started, which proves that a Moebius strip *only has one side.* But if you look at the paper, you'll find pencil markings on both sides. The Moebius strip is a paradox!

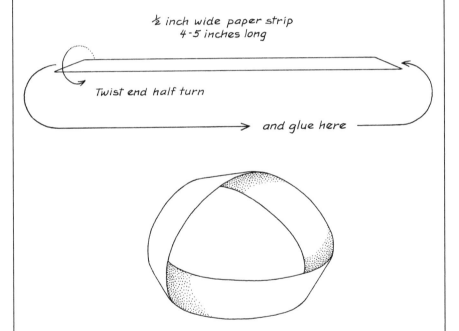

½ inch wide paper strip
4-5 inches long

Twist end half turn

and glue here

The way out of this paradox is to realize that the definition of *side* is important here. Even though the pencil seems to stay on one "side," the fact is there is always a surface on the other "side" of the paper.

1. your past experience with dogs and fleas
2. what you've learned about fleas from your vet or from reading a can of flea powder
3. considering several different approaches, including:
   a. inspecting Fido for fleas
   b. whether or not to send Fido to the kennel for a serious bath
   c. whether to use flea powder or one of those flea collars

Now that last choice—powder or a collar—involves more logic and some background knowledge. Let's say you do some reading about fleas and discover an interesting fact: that fleas need water and make a daily trip to the dog's eyes, where they have a sip. It turns out that somebody who knew that fact and thought about it realized that to get to the eyes, those accursed fleas had to pass by the dog's neck, and from that, the person reasoned that if you put a collar with flea powder around Fido's neck, not only would fleas be killed, any new fleas would be poisoned within twenty-four hours.

So there's a kind of *chain* of logic involved in the simple decision of how to rid a dog of fleas. One conclusion builds on another and, working with your experience and common sense, you can string ideas and link them up to reach pretty complicated, but correct, solutions to problems.

The practical logic diagram shows how logic works in everyday life, how people go about solving problems or figuring out the unknown. Practical logic doesn't follow neat three-sentence patterns like the syllogism. Instead, it looks more like the inner workings of a computer or radio, with connections running here and there. Remember, too, that because each of us has different ways of thinking about things, each person's logic pattern will be somewhat different. Earlier in the chapter I suggested that you draw a map of your own brain, your own thinking style. Obviously that would affect how you go about logically solving problems or explaining the unknown.

How then does logic work in real life? Let's "walk through" a couple of problems to see how a person might solve them. So you *state*

Practical Logic

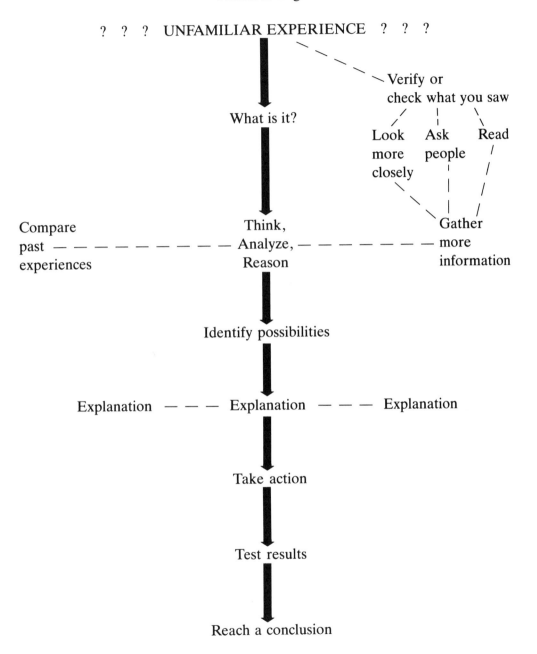

the problem: Fido is scratching a lot and seems uncomfortable. What should we do?

Most pet owners know about fleas from *past experience,* and so you'd probably start guessing right away that Fido has a case of the fleas. You could check that out by *observing* around you, looking for fleas in Fido's fur. Or, if you didn't know what a flea looked like, you might call the vet to *gather more information.* You could also buy some flea powder and read the instructions to see if Fido's symptoms fit the description. You'd probably *check out possibilities,* seeing what you could do for a cure: give him a bath, buy him a flea collar, dust him with flea powder, burn down his doghouse. Eventually you'd *take action* based on your conclusion, and you'd *check it out* to see if you were right: Does the scratching go away? If it does, you'd have logically solved the problem. But if poor Fido continued to hound himself with scratching, you would start all over at the beginning with a new problem, "Fido is still scratching after being treated for fleas."

PROBING ON YOUR OWN

Think about a problem that you've solved or are solving in your life. It might involve building a tree house that doesn't fall out of a tree; it might be getting over an argument with a friend; it could center on solving a story problem in math. Look at the practical logic chart and then draw a diagram or sketch of the parts of your problem. See how you are already using practical logic in your own life.

Now let's take a somewhat more difficult problem. Walking home one evening with your pal Chicken Logician, you are startled by a great glowing light that seems to be hovering over the trees. You hear a deep humming sound, like electrical motors running, and your skin feels tingly. The light remains for about five seconds, then suddenly vanishes. The problem: *What was that?*

As a good practical logician, you'd probably turn to Chicken Logician and say, "Did you see that!?" If Chicken's feathers are extended in all directions and it has a wide-eyed look, you might conclude that Chicken L. has also seen this great light in the sky. You would have *double-checked your observation.*

Next, you'd scan your memory banks for familiar *past experience* only to discover that you've never seen anything like it. This is new. Of course, it might pop into your mind right away that this thing may have been a flying saucer! You wouldn't want to leap to a conclusion, however, so you'd want to *gather more information.* You might phone the police to ask if they'd had any reports or whether they have an explanation. You might guess that this involves electricity, and so you'd call the electric company to see if they had anything going on out your way.

With this problem, drawing a conclusion could be quite difficult. Suppose nobody else saw this great burst of light. The police have no reports of suspicious activity, and the electric company says no, there's nothing going on out there. What could you conclude?

Here one must be very careful with "logic." If you are an avid science-fiction reader and have always dreamed of going on a trip to Mars, you might conclude, "It was a spaceship!" Another person, less inclined to believe in outer spacelings, might conclude: "I must have had too much ice cream—I'm imagining things." An in-between conclusion might be, "I just can't tell on the basis of the evidence."

Could you take action? Perhaps you and Chicken Logician could go on talk shows on TV to describe your otherworldly experience. You might be persuaded that flying saucers *exist,* and that would be action enough. But if that were your conclusion, you'd actually be following a kind of logic that created myths of the supernatural. That's not to say that flying saucers *don't* exist; it's just that one would probably need more information before drawing that conclusion. In the age of myths, people were satisfied with simple, invisible explanations; in our time, a time of modern, practical logic, it takes more to convince us.

Getting Smarter: Training Yourself in Logic

There are books and training courses around that say they will make you smarter or teach you to be a better thinker. I think that the best way for one to get better at thinking is simply to practice it regularly. One of the purposes of this chapter is to alert you to the "big idea" of logic and to encourage you to *think carefully* about what you see and observe. We know much more about the universe than did the ancient believers in myth, magic, and the supernatural, and we are in a position to make better decisions. Because practical logic is so complicated, there are no fixed rules to follow. You just have to practice the skills.

PROBING ON YOUR OWN

Sherlock Holmes's mention of puzzles reminds us that many people enjoy testing their brains with puzzles and games. There are riddles, word problems, cryptograms to be solved; mindbenders to be unbent; paradoxes to be unraveled. Most games involve logic, reason, and problem solving. I've listed several good puzzle books in the bibliography for this chapter, but you can also check your library. You could also pay a visit to a game store near you and ask the clerk to show you some of their logic and reason games. After you've played a number of games like that, you might want to go a step further and create some logic or reason games of your own. Now, that really takes some thinking.

That's pretty much how Sherlock Holmes did it. It would have been easy for Holmes to draw a false conclusion about Dr. Watson's tan and his sore arm. Because he practiced, Holmes got better and better at reaching valid conclusions, to the point that he could dazzle Dr. Watson and millions of readers over the years.

You might take as a personal creed something Holmes said:

> My mind . . . rebels at stagnation. Give me problems, give me work, give me the most abstruse cryptogram or the most intricate analysis, and I am in my own proper atmosphere.

Good thinking!

6

From Myth to Science

Myths are the shadow of the scientist.

—Stephen Larsen

The task of science is both to extend the range of experience and to reduce it to order.

—Neils Bohr

The man who goes beyond appearances is a searcher after truth.

—Francis Huxley

I began this book by showing how myths are one way people go about explaining the world to themselves. But in ordinary language, "myth" has come to mean something that's *not* true, so it was important for us to look at other ways of probing the unknown. We then went on to see how legends, folk culture, superstition, and magic are tied to this same impulse to understand the world. However, they also are linked to the idea of "not true," even though we often find solid elements of truth in them (like folk cures for hiccups). Next I showed how logic and reason can be used to think one's way to explanations that are more satisfactory than, say, myth or magic or superstition. And in this chapter, I'll take you to a topic promised on the cover of the book, to something called science.

"Science" means different things to different people. There are even *mythical* ideas about science, such as the idea that it can solve *any* problem it confronts. You've probably studied a subject called Science in school and know that it can mean anything from studying simple machines such as pulleys and levers to cutting up a deceased frog to see how its innards work. School science often involves studying what scientists have discovered over the years and perhaps checking it out in the laboratory to make certain it's accurate.

On the other hand, if you believe what you see in the movies, you might think that science leads to wild experiments that "go against nature" and threaten the world with strange viruses or mutations. The movie view can give you the idea that scientists can do anything, such as coming up with the antidote to a poison just in the nick of time or rescuing the human race from a mutant bacterial strain created by aliens.

If you read about science in the local newspaper or watch television programs about science, you'll learn of "high tech" developments: smaller and smaller electronic computer chips, microbes that can be "taught" to "eat" the impurities in iron ore, or a breed of "tough" tomatoes that can be harvested by machinery rather than by hand—all products of scientists' working, testing, and probing ideas in the laboratory and out there in the world.

To some people science means all the wonderful gadgetry we have in our homes, from compact disc players to microwave ovens. To others, it is just a great mystery, usually involving test tubes or mathematics, something they'd just as soon not think about or study. To many, science holds out the promise of a better future for Planet Earth, for feeding hungry people, for providing comfortable living for every human being. To still others, science is a threat, leading to destruction of the earth's atmosphere and to mass-produced consumer goods that please the wealthy while the poor fend for themselves.

PROBING ON YOUR OWN

"When I use a word," Humpty Dumpty said, "it means just what I want it to mean—neither more nor less."
—LEWIS CARROLL, *Through the Looking-Glass*

Humpty Dumpty was both right and wrong when he said that a word means just what one wants it to mean. Although each of us has individual ideas about what words mean, it's important for us to agree on definitions so that we can discuss ideas intelligently. This is certainly true with such a broad idea as *science*. What do people mean by *science*? Ask some friends, teachers, adults: "What's your definition of *science*?" "What do scientists do?" "What good is science?" "Do you see anything harmful about it?" Think about the answers to see if you can see any patterns in what people say. In doing so, *you'll* be operating as a scientist—collecting information and drawing conclusions.

What Is **Science?**

The dictionary is of some help in our quest to find out meaning. *Webster's Ninth New Collegiate Dictionary* tells us that the word comes from the Latin word *scire,* meaning simply "to know." The dictionary tells us (not too helpfully) that "science" has to do with "knowledge as distinguished from ignorance" and (more usefully) that it is concerned with "systematized" knowledge and with discovering "general truths" and "general laws." In other words, science involves studying the unknown in an orderly way.

Science engages us in thinking about *ways of knowing,* or *thinking about thinking.* Look at the drawing of the skeleton; it was done by

Andreas Vesalius, a biological artist who lived in Belgium about four hundred years ago. Vesalius was interested in observing the human body and making very accurate drawings of it. I enjoy one of his drawings because it shows a skeleton contemplating a skull, which symbolizes humankind's quest to figure out better and better ways of knowing.

People of science have inquiring minds. They want to know what's going on in the world around them. You don't have to wear a white lab coat to be a scientist, but you do need to be concerned that you're giving things the fullest, best inquiry that you possibly can. Much of this learning is just for the sake of knowing.

Along with the joy of learning, science is concerned with helping people use their understanding to *control* what's going on around them. We use our knowledge of science to predict the weather, to heat houses in wintertime, to bring electricity to light bulbs so we can control the darkness. Stephen Larsen has said that the scientist is like a magician, trying to control the mysterious world. Unlike the magician, the scientist does it with reality rather than illusion. "The scientist," says Larsen, is "the magician of the daylight world."

Perhaps the best description that I have run across for *science* is one offered by Professor Hy Ruchlis: "Science means using one's brains to solve problems for the betterment of humanity, no holds barred."

He is saying that you cannot easily pin down science to a single definition or to a single group of people who study it. Humpty-Dumpty–like, science will involve a variety of approaches to learning by many different people, including you and me. What all views of science have in common is the idea of using the old noodle to come up with ideas that not only make sense, but can be demonstrated to be accurate. I also like the way Professor Ruchlis emphasizes that science should be for the *betterment of humanity*. Science is *not* at its best when it is building bigger and more explosive bombs. Science should be used to help people live better lives, a topic I'll explore in the afterword.

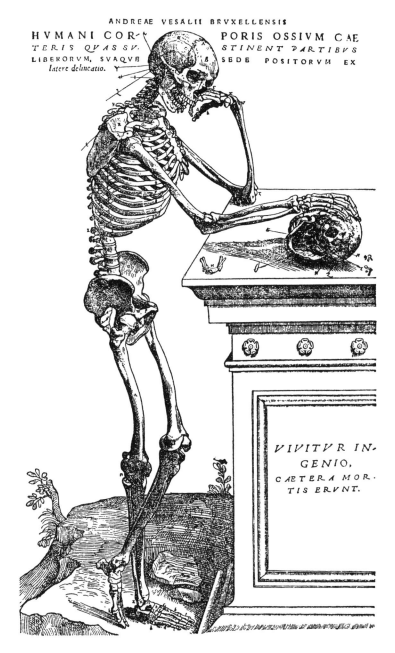

"Thinking About Thinking." From Andreas Vesalius' De Fabrica Humani Corporis, 1543.

The First Scientists

Five thousand years ago, people in Egypt, in the Middle East, and in Asia were trying to make better and better sense of their world. That was an age of myth and superstition, but it was also an age when the impulse toward science was growing. Today, museums around the world have artifacts, objects that have been preserved from those days, to help us understand what the early scientists were doing.

For example, the National Palace Museum in Taiwan, Republic of China, has found evidence that magnetism was recognized as early as 3000 B.C. The Chinese built a magnetic statue that always pointed south. A balance beam, or scale, from the Indus Valley in Asia shows that people were learning more and more about how to weigh and measure things accurately by 2500 B.C. Acupuncture needles, carefully inserted under the skin by Chinese doctors, show that doctor-scientists were exploring the human nervous system in 2300 B.C.

Stonehenge, a circle of gigantic stones in England, was apparently designed to use in taking measurements of the motions of the stars and the planets about 1650 B.C. By 1000 B.C. people had figured out how to melt and blend metals to form new manufactured materials superior to unrefined metals found in nature. By 700 B.C. astronomers had recorded the falling of meteorites and charted a comet, possibly the famous Halley's Comet, which reappears every seventy-six years.

People who study the history of science say that it began "for real" about the seventh century B.C., or 2700 years ago, with the Greeks. Those scientists proposed that the world was made of four basic elements: air, earth, water, and fire. Even though they were wrong, those Greek scientists were on the brink of an amazing idea. Within five hundred years, a Greek named Democritus had figured out an early version of atomic theory, that the world isn't made up just of clouds and birds and animals and rocks, but of tiny particles.

The early scientists didn't work in laboratories and didn't wear white coats. They didn't conduct experiments the way modern scientist do. But they looked out at the world, collected information, thought about what they were seeing, offered explanations, and tried out their ideas, which made them scientists in the best sense.

They were also interested in what some have called the "twin of science," technology, which is the art of translating science into everyday applications. The early scientists figured out how to make perfume and wine; they knew how to plate expensive metals onto cheap metals (which, as you know, supported the alchemists' notion of turning lead into gold); they discovered ways of lifting water from river to field; they learned how to use the stars to chart the seasons and crops, and even how to navigate across bodies of water when you couldn't see the opposite shore.

The early scientists were interested in classifying, too. As they looked around their world, they saw that things had traits in common—animals went with animals, fish with fish, rocks with rocks—and that within those groupings, some fish, say, were more like each other than like other fish. From all this classifying and sorting, they came to a fuller understanding of how the world was made up of families of things.

A Breakthrough: The Orderly Universe

The time of early science must have been exciting because there were so many different ideas of what was going on in the universe. Many people believed in a world where gods and goddesses were in control. Magicians, oracles, and sorcerers claimed to have power over that unseen world. At the same time, some philosophers were working to make knowledge more systematic, so logic was beginning to develop right alongside science and myth and magic and superstition.

A great change in thinking happened at that time. Scientists recognized that the world followed patterns. If you studied, you could detect those patterns and from them reach reliable conclusions. Now, that may seem pretty obvious to us today, but in an age when supernatural forces were supposed to be in control, this was an important

PROBING ON YOUR OWN

Classifying is basic to science. To get a feel for how it works, pick twenty-five small objects from your home and put them in a bag. You might choose a spoon and a cookie from the kitchen, a pencil and a piece of paper from a desk, a stuffed animal and a dirty sock from your room, a nail and a bottle of glue from a work area. Then, on a clear surface, free from other stuff, remove objects from the bag and try to sort them into piles based on similarities. You might, for example, put all soft things in one pile and hard things in another. Or you might sort things into big, small, and in between. You might sort objects based on whether they're used for work or for play. You can rearrange your stuff into many different piles.

Finally, sort the objects into piles that you think would tell a stranger, an intelligent visitor from outer space, the most about *you.*

In a sense, that's what the scientist's classifications are all about. The scientist wants to sort the stuff of the universe into "piles" or categories that will tell the most about the universe itself.

breakthrough. These thinkers helped to establish several rules about the world that we essentially still use as a basis for scientific study today:

They figured out that the world is orderly. That is, they realized that things seem to happen in the same way over and over: *Seasons come and go, but they repeat. If you drop a rock, it falls. If you drop a rock on your thumb, the thumb is hurt. When the sky gets cloudy, it usually rains.*

They figured out that you can measure and keep records about the universe. If you take measurements and collect information, eventually you can make some generalizations or theories about what's going on. *All objects are made out of air, earth, fire, or water. The earth is the center of the universe, and the stars circle around it.* Not all of those early theories were correct. (The two I just gave you are both wrong.) However, it would be from more measuring and record keeping that newer, more accurate theories would arise.

They figured out that theories could be tested. If your observations were accurate and the stars were "favorable," you could plant at a certain time of year and get a good crop. If you understood how water flowed, you could build a pump to get water to flow where you wanted it to go.

PROBING ON YOUR OWN

As I've said, the early scientists didn't always come up with correct answers. They were wrong when they said that the earth was the center of the universe, and they were wrong when they concluded that it was "built" from air, earth, water, and fire. But it's easy to be wrong in making scientific conclusions, especially if, like the early scientists, you don't have the benefit of all the knowledge at our disposal today.

To understand this, imagine that all your knowledge is based totally on what you can gather with your own senses. You have no books to tell you what things are like, no television to show you faraway places. You *must* base your conclusions on the evidence you can collect yourself. Answer the following questions:

- Is the earth round or flat?
- How many religions are there?
- Who is the supreme ruler?
- How many languages are there?
- Where is the center of the universe?

On the basis of our limited vision, most of us would come up with *wrong* answers to those questions!

The Birth of Experimental Science

Eventually, people became even more systematic about science and learning. About 1600, just four hundred years ago, Englishman Francis Bacon wrote about the "advancement of learning." He worried that people often deceive themselves about the world. When we talk about knowledge, Bacon said, it's as if we were sitting inside a cave and giving a lecture on what the rest of the world is like.

In France, a writer named René Descartes (pronounced day-*cart,* with a silent "s") went so far as to say that he wasn't certain that he could even prove that he himself was real. He got out of that mess by saying something you'll hear quoted many times: "I think; therefore I am." His best-known book had the long title *Discourse on Method: To Properly Conduct Reason and to Search for the Truth in the Science.* Descartes wanted to guarantee that when scientists said they had found "truth," they had taken precautions to make certain they weren't just describing their own imagination or wishful thinking.

For example, he argued that scientists should break problems into small pieces and look at those bits one by one. If you could discover small truths, eventually you could put the evidence and theories together to get to bigger and bigger ideas. Descartes also set up guidelines to help people avoid error.

From the thinking of people like Bacon and Descartes came what we have come to call "the scientific method." Its stages are shown in the box. You begin by *stating a problem* or asking the question you want to answer. Next you *collect data,* gathering information that will help you figure out the answer. After a time, after you've collected enough info, you *form a hypothesis* or a hunch about your problem. Finally, you *test the hypothesis* to see whether or not it was correct.

Another Englishman, Thomas Henry Huxley, later explained the idea of how the scientific method worked:

> Suppose you go into a fruiterer's shop, wanting an apple—you take up one, and, on biting it, you find it is sour; you look at it,

THE SCIENTIFIC METHOD

Step One: *Identify the problem or question.*

Example: What causes rain?

Step Two: *Collect data or information.*

Examples: Study weather patterns. Examine what goes on when it has rained in the past. Take measurements of air pressure, temperature, other elements of the weather.

Step Three: *Create a hypothesis or theory.*

Example: Rain is caused by saturation of the air with water vapor, so that when the temperature and pressure are right, the water condenses to create rain.

Step Four: *Test the hypothesis.*

Example: Collect *much* more data on weather and rain. See if you can predict accurately when it will rain and when it won't rain.

Note: The question "What causes rain?" is really too broad for true scientific research. Weatherpeople have been trying to figure it out for years, and as you know, weather forecasts are not always accurate. In actual research, a scientist would probably narrow down the topic quite a bit, focusing on a single aspect of rain, like why it rains so much in Buffalo, New York, or whether you can predict sprinkles *versus* a cloudburst.

and see that it is hard and green. You take up another one, and that too is hard, green, and sour. The shopman offers you a third, but, before biting it, you examine it, and find it is hard and green, and you immediately say that you will not have it, as it must be sour, like those you have already tried.

In this case you identified a problem ("I want an apple"), collected data (tasting two apples), and created a hypothesis ("Hard green apples are sour"). Mr. Huxley went on to say that your hypothesis might well be true for the remaining apples in that fruit store. You wouldn't need to take a bite out of every apple in the store, but would simply say, "No, thanks, I don't want to buy these." But you'd make a big mistake if you said, "I'll never eat another hard green apple in my life, because they're all sour." You'd probably want to run more tests. You might go to another fruiterer's shop, try the hard greenies, and see how they taste. In fact, some green-skinned, firm apples taste quite sweet. In any case, as a cautious, "scientific" thinker, you'd continue to test your hypothesis, even though you wouldn't buy any hard, green apples from fruiterer number 1.

You might say that Thomas Huxley's example is just common sense, and he would agree. He said that most of us use the scientific method in our everyday lives to solve problems systematically. (At the same time, Huxley, like Francis Bacon, warned not to trust that common sense too closely.)

Let's imagine the scientific method at work in a modern lab, say the laboratory at a county agricultural center that helps farmers grow crops more effectively. As an apple farmer, you discover your best-selling apple, the Sweet Greenie, is turning diseased. There's a *problem:* What's causing the disease? You bring in a bushel of Sweet Greenies, and the scientist at the lab looks at them under a lens. The scientist quickly sees that there are all kinds of tiny insects on the diseased apples, some bugs that he or she has never seen before.

Now, the obvious answer to the problem might be to say that the bugs are causing the disease and then to look for a poison that would kill them. However, the scientist in the lab asks a question:

"Did you get these from the tree or pick them up off the ground?"

You explain that you just scooped them off the ground, looking for the diseased ones.

Instead of giving you a prescription for bug killer, the scientist sends you back for more apples.

"This time," he or she says, "pick a bushel off one tree, both diseased and healthy apples. Then go to another part of the orchard and collect a second bushel the same way."

The scientist is collecting more data to make certain that you're getting a clear picture of what's going on. It could be that the first batch you brought in had picked up the bugs only after the apples had fallen to the ground. After looking at the more careful sample, the scientist could work toward pinning down the problem more accurately. We'll leave the story there and assume that, in time, the scientist will figure out the problem of the diseased Sweet Greenies and save your crop.

Scientific method, then, is not a simple four-step process that magically produces right answers. It takes a lot of work, investigation, thinking, and rethinking. It requires the ability to keep on looking for better answers after you thought you had a problem all figured out.

PROBING ON YOUR OWN

Try deliberately applying the scientific method in your own life. Select a small problem that has been troubling you. It might be a question: "Who's been squeezing the toothpaste tube from the top?" It might be a mechanical difficulty: "My skateboard seems to pull to the left." It might be an annoyance: "When I'm trying to study, my little brother's loud radio blasts through the wall and distracts me." For whatever problem, collect information, form a hypothesis, and test it out. This could lead you to nab the toothpaste culprit, tighten a screw in your skateboard, or ask your brother to move his radio to the other side of his room.

The Scientific Revolution

The ideas of people like Francis Bacon and René Descartes took the world by storm, and "science" has captured the imagination of the world ever since. What really helped to sell the idea of science, however, was a series of discoveries made by sixteenth- and seventeenth-century scientists that demonstrated what could happen when one approached explaining the unknown scientifically. These discoveries focused on no less a question than "Where in the universe are we?"

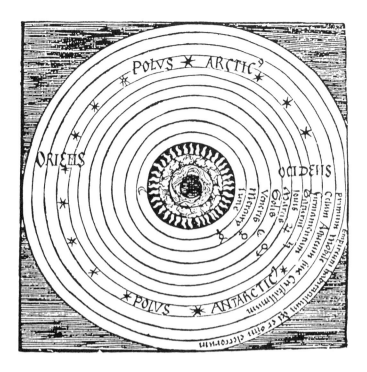

The geocentric view of the solar system. Geocentric *means "earth-centered."*
The drawing shows the solar system as visualized by the philosopher/scientist
Aristotle. At the center is earth, which Aristotle saw as being made up of air,
earth, water, and fire. The next rings are the planets and the stars. On the very
outside of the diagram are shown the dwellings of the gods, so you can see
that Aristotle's universe included both myth and science.

The myths of many nations place the earth at the center of the
universe, with the sky, stars, and sun wrapped around it. Ordinary
common sense agrees. So did the Greek scientists, who hypothesized
that the sun, stars, and planets travel in circular orbits about our
earth. However, as they collected more and more information, they
noticed some oddities, such as the fact that the planets don't always
appear in the same relationship to one another in the sky. Nor do the
planets show up at the same places in the constellations, which you'd
expect if the sky were like a dome over the earth. Most of the Greek
scientists believed in a geocentric, or earth-centered, universe, and
they just dismissed the irregularities. One astronomer, Ptolemy (*Toh-
luh-me*), was especially influential and developed a complicated idea

of "epicycles," orbits within orbits, to explain the data that didn't fit quite right.

At least one Greek astronomer, Aristarchus, disagreed. In about 270 B.C. he argued that the epicycles could be explained more satisfactorily if you realized that the sun, not the earth, was the center of the solar system. However, his ideas were ignored. (Often right ideas are ignored just because they aren't in tune with the old way of thinking.)

In 1543, almost eighteen hundred years after Aristarchus, a Polish astronomer named Nicholas Copernicus presented a heliocentric, or sun-centered, view of the world. In the spirit of the new science, he rejected the old hypothesis and was quite critical of the work of people like Ptolemy. He wrote:

> They were so uncertain about the motion of the Sun and Moon that they could not demonstrate or observe the unvarying lengths of the yearly cycle. Then, in setting out the motions of the Sun and Moon and of the five other planets, they did not in each case employ the same principles, assumptions, and demonstrations.

The older scientists, in short, even used conflicting explanations of the universe in order to cling to their earth-centered theory. Copernicus added, "It began to vex me." Using fresh observations and mathematics, he worked out a system with the sun at the center of things. You may have noticed that Copernicus referred to *five* planets, rather than the nine that we know about today. He didn't have telescopes available for his work, so all his wonderful calculations were based essentially on looking at the stars with the naked eye.

However, telescopes were in the works, as scientists were busily developing new tools to help them measure the universe more precisely. The creation of the telescope enabled another astronomer, Galileo, to report that he could confirm the Copernican theory. Peering through his telescope, Galileo was able to offer the solid scientific evidence that Copernicus's theory was correct. Both Copernicus and

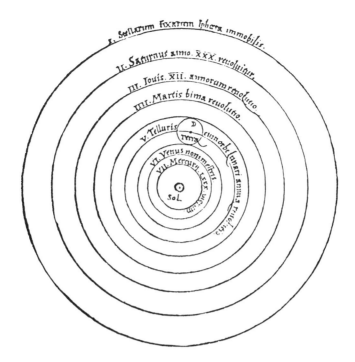

The heliocentric view of the solar system. Here is a drawing of the solar system according to Nicholas Copernicus. The sun is at the center, with the planets around it. Earth is the third planet out. The outside circle represents the stars. (Taylor, 1949, p. 73)

Galileo took a great deal of heat for their new theory. They were accused of trying to upset the old order of things.

Despite the "correctness" of the new theory, however, both Copernicus and Galileo held on to at least one old idea that proved wrong. They assumed that the planets traveled in orbits that were perfect circles. Neither man could break free from that idea, despite the fact that not all of their evidence quite fit the perfect circle idea.

It took yet another scientist, Johannes Kepler, to figure out that the planets were traveling in oval (or elliptical) orbits around the sun. If one took that into account, many of the irregularities that we see from our station on Planet Earth could be explained quite naturally.

And beyond Kepler, another famous scientist-astronomer-mathemetician, Isaac Newton, developed a mathematical explanation for the ways in which the planets were traveling. To test his theory as well as the math he had developed to go with it, Newton calculated the orbits of the planets. In 1687 he published a book called *Mathematical Principles of Natural Philosophy* explaining these ideas, 144 years after Copernicus had first explained the heliocentric universe.

You can see, then, that this "scientific revolution" didn't take place instantly. It required a number of people (and not only the science superstars I've listed here) to develop and refine the view of the universe and to develop the details of the scientific method. That work goes on to this day. In the days since Newton, scientists have probed every part of the unknown, from the tiny worlds of molecules and viruses to the vastness of outer space. They've looked into the atmosphere above us and the seas below in the quest for knowledge. They have figured out how to capture some of the power of the universe, and they have used that power, in turn, to bring about improvements in our way of life: heat, light, communications.

Using much more refined measuring devices, and employing more and more complicated computers and mathematical formulas, scientists continue to question and probe, to reject old theories that don't work, to develop new ones, to quest after explanations for the unknown.

Science and the Jigsaw Puzzle of Knowledge

The wonderful discoveries of science sometimes make us forget that it also involves an enormous amount of hard work, and even a little bit of luck.

Some important scientific discoveries have been made quite by accident. Charles Goodyear, whose name adorns the blimp, discovered a process of "vulcanization" of rubber by accident. He was experimenting with natural rubber, trying to make it less brittle, when some boiled over on his kitchen stove. The stuff that cooked onto the stove surface had the very properties he wanted. You can see that his actual discovery was not very methodical, but it's also true that like a good scientist, Goodyear knew what he was looking for and was trying to find answers systematically.

Scientific inquiry is full of false starts and dead ends. Sometimes scientists discover that they defined the problem wrongly in the first place, or that what they saw as the problem was actually a part of a bigger problem. Sometimes Descartes's advice of breaking a problem into small pieces doesn't work, because the whole is simply bigger than all the little parts put together. There are times, too, when following the scientific method just doesn't work, when people collect lots of data and just don't come up with any answers. There are even times when solving a problem "scientifically" creates an even bigger problem. For example, we're just discovering that chemicals that scientifically controlled insects decades ago left harmful residues in the food chain that will be with us forever.

As an example of the complexity of modern science, we can look at a single "problem": The world seems to be getting hotter. Although we can give this problem a label, the "greenhouse effect," it is enormously complicated. Some scientists argue that so much carbon dioxide is being produced by our factories and our cars that the earth's atmosphere is holding on to heat. Other theorists observe that because forests are being chopped down all over the world, we're losing Mother Nature's power to reconvert the carbon dioxide into oxygen. Other factors are involved: There's a theory that the chemicals used in aerosol spray cans enter the atmosphere and destroy ozone, a chemical that helps to protect or insulate the earth from the sun's ultraviolet rays. Another theory holds that by-products of plastic products also destroy the ozone. Along with those theories, some conflicting evidence seems to show not that the earth is getting hotter but that we are in a temporary warming cycle.

Even predictions about what a greenhouse effect would mean differ rather widely. Some researchers say that a warming trend on the earth would melt the polar ice caps, leading to flooding all around the earth. Other theories state that because of the warming and evaporation, the earth would dry up, leading to vast areas of desert. Computers have been programmed to test out these theories, but given current information, any one of those predictions might prove correct.

The greenhouse effect, then, poses for modern scientists a problem that is every bit as complicated and fascinating as "Where in the solar system are we?" And it's a problem that may take at least the next 144 years to work out.

I hope you can see, then, that science isn't something neat and clean that can drive away all the myths and superstition in the world and lead to magic solutions to our problems. In fact, writer Vivian Gornick has created a fascinating example of what science can be at its puzzling best:

> Imagine . . . that you have a printed jigsaw puzzle with no picture printed on it. All you have is pieces and you haven't a clue how to make sense of it. The pieces are your separate scientific observations.

Science has to take those plain pieces and twist and turn them, trying different possibilities, until everything fits together.

In fact, everything I have written about in this book is a part of that same puzzle, isn't it? Whether we're discussing myths of powerful giants or bad-boy tricksters, ways of curing warts, magic that defies the senses, logical explanations of fleas or tortoises, or figuring out a new computer chip in the laboratory, we're puzzling over the nature of our universe. Sometimes it's a puzzle we can solve quickly on our own; sometimes it's exploring a vast puzzle that may take many members of the human race many lifetimes to figure out. There certainly are some puzzles that we'll *never* be able to solve.

I might add that the puzzle on which we're working is one that has no limits. The edges of the unknown are even greater than our remarkable powers of imagination. There will always be at least one more piece to fit into the jigsaw puzzle we've called **probing the unknown.**

Afterword: Future Knowledge

Over four hundred years have passed since the "scientific revolution" in which Copernicus, Galileo, and Isaac Newton changed the idea of how the universe is set up and, in the process, changed the whole concept of science. During those four hundred years, scientists have looked everyplace they could think of for information about the world. Their discoveries have revolutionized the world so that we live in an age of science. In fact, when we talk about science, we often use words like *magical, wondrous, spectacular.* It has even been said that science has become a new mythology, the modern myth being that if you use the scientific method, you *always* get results. Scientists have taken the place of the wizards and witch doctors and alchemists of yore, with extraordinary powers over the forces of the universe.

The Accomplishments of Science

The discoveries of scientists are as much a part of our lives as the air we breathe. In fact, our understanding of the breath of life itself comes from science. We confidently tell one another that we breathe in something called oxygen (along with other gases) and exhale carbon dioxide. We explain that the oxygen acts with body fuels—

food—to create energy for our bodies to function. How do we know that? Have you ever *seen* oxygen or carbon dioxide? How do you know what happens inside your body when oxygen and "fuels" combine?

Much of our knowledge of breathing comes from the work of scientists who followed Isaac Newton and who scientifically disproved some older Greek ideas about respiration. Robert Boyle (who lived from 1627 to 1691) trapped gases and figured out what makes them expand and contract. Antoine Lavoisier (1743–1794) learned how to isolate oxygen in the laboratory and learned about its properties. Joseph Priestley (1733–1804) first learned how to "capture" carbon dioxide and figured out some of the things it does in the human bloodstream. From these scientists, and thousands and thousands of others, we have learned the details of a world of respiration that most of us have never actually seen!

Another unseen world that science has discovered for us has to do with the structure of everything in the universe. We know—as did some of the Greeks—that the world is not quite what it seems, that it is made up of tiny particles. We know of molecules, which are made up of tinier particles, called atoms, which are themselves made up of even smaller particles called neutrons and protons and electrons (and particles even smaller than those!). But who has actually seen a molecule or an atom? How can we be sure that we're not confusing ourselves, believing superstitiously in an atomic world of imaginary particles?

Our confidence in the world of atoms comes to us through a string of scientists, including John Dalton (1766–1846), who was the first to figure out the structure of atoms; Marie Curie (1867–1934), who explored radium and researched the curious properties that made it send off invisible rays; Max Planck (1858–1947), who figured out a mathematical quantum theory to explain the energy levels in atoms; and Albert Einstein (1879–1955), who was able to explain the connection between atoms and energy, which knowledge, for better or worse, helped unleash the nuclear power inside atoms.

Your life expectancy—how old you can expect, on the average, to live—is greater than that of anybody who has ever lived on earth. Whereas four hundred years ago the average life expectancy was about forty years, you can confidently expect to live to be in your high seventies. You owe your lifespan in part to scientists such as Louis Pasteur (1822–1895), who did important research into microbes (*micro*scopic *b*iological organisms) and how to control them, or Ignaz Semmelweiss (1818–1865), who promoted the use of clean hospital practices to defeat invisible germs that few people believed in.

We know a great deal about a story nobody observed firsthand: the story of how human beings evolved on earth. It's a story that has been figured out by such scientists as Charles Darwin (1809–1882), who developed the idea that plants and animals evolve over long periods; Gregor Mendel (1822–1884), who discovered the patterns by which the characteristics of plants and animals are passed from one generation to the next; Francis Crick and James Watson, who in 1953 announced that they had discovered the structure of a molecule called DNA that is responsible for determining the characteristics living things will have.

Science has had an amazing string of victories and discoveries about heat, light, energy, motion, the stars, the planets, small worlds, vast universes. The wonders of science have become so amazing that apparently wild dreams often come true. In doing his research, Isaac Newton supposed that if you fired a cannonball off a mountain with enough speed, you could actually get it to travel around the earth; in our day, satellites float in orbit, taking weather photographs and transmitting television pictures and telephone conversations, achievements far beyond what Newton predicted.

One hundred years ago, Jules Verne wrote a book called *Twenty Thousand Leagues Under the Sea* about an amazing boat that could travel beneath the water for long periods of time. In our time, we not only have submarines, but nuclear-powered subs—the first one named *Nautilus* after the undersea craft in Jules Verne's book. About the same time, science-fiction writer H. G. Wells predicted not only flight, but aerial warfare. (Let's hope his prediction of a *War of the Worlds* between Martians and Earthlings *doesn't* come true!)

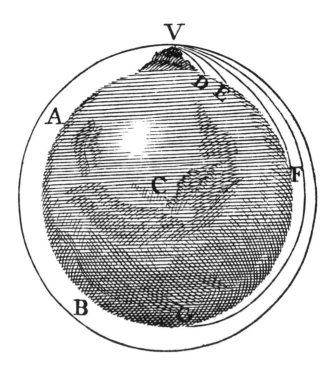

Newton's satellite. The sketch shows a mountaintop (V), from which a cannon is fired. If the cannon is fired with too little powder, the cannonball will drop to earth (D,E,F,G). But if you put in enough powder, you could put the cannonball into orbit (A, B). In actuality, it would not be possible to build a gunpowder cannon strong enough to launch a cannonball, but we've done the next best thing by developing rockets that are capable of launching earth satellites. From Newton's System of the World, 1728. Reprinted by permission of the Houghton Library, Harvard University.

When science-fiction writers today talk about travel to other planets, about freezing sick people to be cured in the future, about telephones with pictures, or about computers that talk or even write down what you say, they are often describing accomplishments of science that are in the works right now!

Looking to the Future

Science is becoming even more sophisticated, thanks in no small measure to an electronic revolution that has brought computers into the laboratory. Computers keep getting faster, larger (in terms of capacity), smaller (in physical size), allowing scientists to take measurements that allow them to probe ever more deeply into unknown worlds.

For example, the whole area of "computer visualization" lets scientists flex their imaginations in exciting new ways. Programmed properly, a computer can digest information and translate it into pictures, even pictures that are predictions of the future. Scientists are now using computers to see what will happen to a dying star over the next

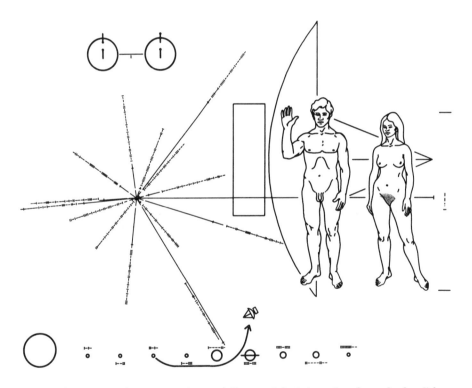

When the National Aeronautics and Space Administration launched a "deep space" probe, Pioneer II, *it attached a plaque with a sketch of human beings and a map showing the origin of the spacecraft from earth. The idea was simply that if beings from another part of the universe find* Pioneer II, *they can make sense of this wordless message. The plaque thus symbolizes what we have accomplished with science, but it holds out as well the science-fiction idea of creatures from outer space. From* Space Pioneers and Where They Are Now *(National Aeronautics and Space Administration, 1987).*

PROBING ON YOUR OWN

Marshall McLuhan, a Canadian professor, once wrote, "One thing about which a fish knows nothing is water." He wanted to warn people that, like fish, we often take familiar things for granted (just as we take it for granted that it's oxygen that we breathe and that when we wake up tomorrow, there will be plenty of it for us to suck into our lungs). Science is one of those things we've come to take for granted.

To raise your own awareness, spend a day (or even part of a day) thinking about all the ways science touches your life. For example, when you have your bowl of cornflakes, read the label on the package to see the scientific analysis of ingredients; think about the complex machines (which are based on discoveries of science) that make those cornflakes; consider the printing press that created the brightly colored box and what the art of printing owes to science; think about the milk you pour on those flakes of corn (milk that has been "pasteurized" by a process developed through Louis Pasteur's research to guarantee that it is safe to drink).

Or flip through the newspaper and look for signs of science. Consider how the front-page news, which may be from Washington or London or Tokyo, got to the newspaper through communications networks, including satellites. Look at the advertisements for gadgets such as computers and car phones and refrigerators and think about the science that created them.

Throughout your day, whether it's on a bus on your way to school (a bus powered by an amazing product of science and technology called the internal combustion engine) or sitting at your desk (Look at the plastic surface, the metal legs—how did science help to create them?) or sitting around watching TV (How did we get pictures that fly through the air to your set?), become more aware of the "water" in which we "swim": the sea of science.

billion years, to guess at what will happen to a piece of metal that is put under stress a million times, to design new cars and "test" how they will work, to estimate how a cornfield will grow under the influence of different soils and fertilizers. Through computer visualization, projects that used to require hundreds or thousands of hours in a laboratory can be done in just a few minutes.

Sophisticated measuring devices on satellites and space probes keep giving us more and more information about the past and future of the planet on which we live. Space probes to Venus may tell us more about how the earth was formed and what may happen to earth if the greenhouse effect continues. Probes to Mars will go so close and make such incredibly precise measurements that we'll settle for certain the old question of whether or not there is life on Mars.

Some of the new applications of computers sound like the science-fiction stories of yesterday. Computers have learned to "read," so they can recognize print (and sometimes handwriting) and record words from a page. Some computers can "talk," and voice synthesizers have led to talking elevators, talking subway trains (run by computers, not human beings), even talking soft-drink machines. Some computers can recognize spoken words, and it appears to be only a matter of time before computers can routinely recognize most words spoken to them. When that happens, you'll be able to dictate a

"Mr. Boffo" by Joe Martin. Reprinted by permission of Tribune Media Services.

report or story to a computer, and it will print out a nice clean copy of what you said, with any grammatical errors corrected.

Even using the library, which is really a good way to learn about the unknown, is changing under the influence of computers. Because of their great speed and convenience, computers are being used to store all kinds of information. Today if you want to learn about a topic, you can go to a computer terminal in a library, type in what you're looking for, wait a few seconds, and get a printout telling you all the books that the library has on that topic. Tomorrow, the old familiar card catalog at the library will disappear, replaced by a computer that will locate information for you very rapidly. Even whole books will be stored in computer memories rather than on paper, and "old-fashioned" books will disappear. You'll just do your reading from a computer screen. In fact, you may not have to travel to the library at all; you'll be able to punch in what you want at the console of your home computer and the library will "download" what you want.

Another science-fiction dream is also coming true—the idea of artificial intelligence (AI): computers that *think*. Most computer scientists doubt that we'll ever develop a computer that can do original thinking. Computers may never have the magic "spark" of human intelligence that lets us make great leaps in thinking or follow hunches or intuition. However, it's clear that we can build computers that can imitate human thinking so closely that you won't be certain whether you're working with a person or a machine. We probably won't see the science-fiction nightmare of a computer ruling the world, but we will see more and more computers making decisions that were formerly made by human beings. This will be a world where computers do more and more of the routine thinking and information processing, freeing up human beings for more creative thought.

The future of knowing looks very bright indeed. We have at our fingertips the power to acquire more knowledge about the universe more quickly than any group of people previously living on this planet. Although we'll never know *everything* we want to know about the unknown, some of earth's greatest mysteries remain to be solved, and likely will be solved, by future generations of thinkers.

PROBING ON YOUR OWN

In a wonderful book, *The Mysterious World,* Francis Hitching has prepared an "Atlas of the Unexplained," a listing of some of the world's mysteries that have never been satisfactorily explained. Some of these will be figured out in the future, some may not be. You might enjoy getting his book or reading up on some of the following mysteries of the unknown:

What killed off the dinosaurs?

How did life originate on earth?

Is there life on other planets—in our solar system or in other universes?

What makes birds migrate? How do they know where they're going?

Can animals "think"? Do any animals have language?

Who discovered America?

Were there ever dragons? Could they fly?

Why do so many ships disappear near the "Bermuda Triangle"?

"Broom-Hilda" by Russell Myers. Reprinted by permission of Tribune Media Services.

Dangers and Warning Signals

Despite all the amazing advances of science, we're also worried about what's happening in our world as a result of "progress." Science isn't magic; it doesn't come up with *all* the answers; and sometimes its answers create more problems than they solve.

For example, thirty years ago, scientists figured out that a particularly strong species of fish could be introduced into Africa's Lake Victoria, the lake that is the source of the Nile River. The idea was that these fish, which often grow to be over two hundred pounds, would be a good source of food and of recreation. They did, indeed, love their new home, so much so that they have created very complicated problems. In the first place, these are very hungry fish, even known to eat their own young. As they grow in number, they are squeezing out other kinds of fish in Lake Victoria, including some valuable species that are found nowhere else in the world. The big fish may have wiped out another fish that eats the microscopic algae in the lake. As a result, algae (the green "scum" you sometimes see on ponds) are covering the lake and using up its valuable oxygen supplies. Beyond that, building the factories to process the giant fish has led to the chopping down of many forests. That has, in turn, increased the runoff of waste water into Lake Victoria, which has further stimulated the algae growth and led to even more depletion of the oxygen. A "simple" idea—"Let's stock the lake with new fish"— has proved to have complex, harmful side effects.

This sort of story is becoming more and more common in the world. An apparently harmless form of plastic used in the cups at fast-food restaurants has turned out to be partly responsible for the loss of ozone in the air above the Antarctic, and that, in turn, is contributing to the greenhouse effect. Chemicals that were used successfully to increase our food supply are now found to be harmful to human beings and to be locked permanently into our food chain. Attempts to irrigate dry lands have led to successful farming, but they have also led to such a population increase in those areas that the lakes have gone dry.

The list goes on:

• That wonderful invention, the automobile, has also brought about pollution of the earth's atmoshere.

• The release of energy from the atom, which offers the promise of a boundless supply of energy, has also given us nuclear wastes that are tough to get rid of, nuclear accidents that can irradiate thousands of people, and nuclear weapons that can destroy the world hundreds of times over.

• Computers, which give us the ability to make great discoveries and gain access to deep piles of information, also can lead to an invasion of our privacy because the computer can store so much information about our personal lives. Computers can also give us "information overload," in which we get so much material that we can't understand it. And you've no doubt heard about computer "thieves," who use their knowledge of computer networks to steal—money, secrets, valuable information.

• Robots that can be programmed to do a lot of heavy work in industry also put people out of work and add to unemployment.

Now, science is not to blame for these problems. Science may have developed plastic, but it didn't create the fast-food restaurants that spawned all the ozone-killing trash. Science may have shown that giant fish can grow in Lake Victoria, but it was people—sport fishermen, in fact—who actually put them into the lake. Nor can we blame the atomic bomb on the people who first figured out how to split the atom.

But there is a real worry nowadays that science is out of control, that it's almost too much of a good thing. We now have the power in our hands to destroy the earth through bombs or pollution; we actually have the power to end human life itself.

Science and Responsibility

Many people are now saying that we have to take a look at what becomes of our discoveries. Erich Fromm, a psychologist, has said that in itself, science is "neutral"; it merely offers discoveries. The real worry, Fromm feels, is how people go about using the new discoveries. It's *our* choice, he says, whether we want to build nuclear bombs or nuclear power stations. It's *our* decision as to whether we want to make more cars and live in a polluted world. *We* have to decide whether we want computers to serve us or whether we will become slaves to them.

Erich Fromm says it's very important for people to understand what's going on in science, to know about the newest in knowledge. He adds that people must also be committed to making certain that discoveries are used to improve humankind's lot, not wreck it.

Just as the discoveries of science could be used to destroy the earth, science could also be put to work solving the world's most pressing problems. Think of the possibilities if we put our energies to work on such problems as:

- getting the earth's population under control
- feeding starving people all over the world
- controlling disease
- making life more comfortable for more people
- ending wars
- improving communications among all people on earth

Erich Fromm called his book *The Revolution of Hope,* for he felt that the future is a positive one if people think hard about what's good in life and make certain that knowledge is used in the service of humanity.

I dedicated this book to "noodle users everywhere"—to people who like to think and puzzle about the unknown. It's the noodle users who can make the difference as to whether we use our knowledge to push ourselves to a bright and optimistic future or into a dark and frightening unknown.

References

*Recommended for young adult readers.

CHAPTER ONE: **Legends and Myths**

Barmé, Geremie, ed. *Lazy Dragon: Chinese Stories from the Ming Dynasty*. Hong Kong: Joint Publishing Company, 1981.

*Brunvald, Jan Harold. *The Vanishing Hitchhiker*. New York: W. W. Norton, 1981.

Colum, Padraic. *Story Telling: Old and New*. New York: Macmillan, 1968.

Gayley, Charles Mills, ed. *Classic Myths in English Literature*. Boston: Ginn and Company, 1893.

*Graham, Judith. *Hawaiian Voices*. Honolulu, HI: Bess Press, 1982.

Grimal, Pierre, ed. *Larousse World Mythology*. New York: G. P. Putnam's, 1965.

*Gringhuis, Kirk. *Lore of the Great Turtle*. Mackinac Island, MI: Mackinac Island State Park Commission, 1970.

*Hayes, Joe. *Coyote & xxxxx*. Santa Fe, NM: Trails West Publishing, 1983. Cassette.

Leeming, David. *Mythology*. New York: Newsweek Books, 1976.

Lowry, Shirley Park. *Familiar Mysteries*. New York: Oxford University Press, 1982.

Mercantante, Anthony. *Good and Evil*. New York: Harper & Row, 1978.

Radin, Paul. *The Trickster*. New York: Bell, 1956.

*Robinson, Herbert Spencer, ed. *Myths and Legends of All Nations*.

Totowa, NJ: Littlefield, Adams, 1976. Also available in paperback from Bantam Books.

*Sproul, Gloria C. *Mishe-Mokwa and the Legend of Sleeping Bear.* Greenwich, CT: Mishe-Mokwa Publishing, 1979.

*   *The Enchanted Worlds: The Book of Beginnings.* Alexandria, VA: Time-Life Books, 1986.

CHAPTER TWO: The Spirit World

Bardens, Dennis. *Ghosts and Hauntings.* New York: Taplinger, 1965.

*Bird, Malcolm. *The Witch's Handbook.* New York: St. Martin's, 1984.

*Blundell, Nigel, and Roger Boar. *The World's Greatest Ghosts.* London: Octopus Books, 1983.

Brode, Anthony. *Haunted Hampshire.* Newbury, Berkshire, England: Countryside Books, 1981.

*Canning, John, ed. *Fifty Great Ghost Stories.* London: Souvenir Press, 1971.

*Cohen, Daniel. *The Encyclopedia of Ghosts.* New York: Dodd, Mead, 1984.

*Conan Doyle, Sir Arthur. *The Hound of the Baskervilles.* London: John Murray and Jonathan Cape, 1974.

Green, Andrew. *Ghosts of Today.* London: Kaye and Ward, 1980.

Hacker, David. "Old Inn's Owners Claim Some Ghastly Goings On," *Detroit Free Press* (October 28, 1988) 1A, 14A.

*Haining, Peter. *The Complete Ghost Stories of Charles Dickens.* London: Michael Joseph, 1982.

*———. *Ghosts: The Illustrated History.* New York: Macmillan, 1975.

"Haunted London: A Ghost Walk." Streets of London Tours, July 21, 1988.

Hole, Christina. *Haunted England.* London: B. T. Batsford, 1949.

Larsen, Stephen. *The Shaman's Doorway: Opening the Mythic Imagination.* New York: Harper & Row, 1976.

Lethbridge, T. C. *Ghost and Divining Rod.* London: Routledge & Kegan Paul, 1963.

Norman, Diana. *The Stately Ghosts of England.* New York: Dorsett, 1963.

*Schwartz, Alvin. *In a Dark, Dark Room.* New York: Harper & Row, 1984.

*———. *Scary Stories to Tell in the Dark.* New York: Lippincott, 1984.

Sergeant, Philip W. *Historic British Ghosts.* East Ardsley, Yorkshire, England: E. P. Publishing, 1974.

*Sutherland, Jon, and Simon Farrell. *Haunted Houses.* London: MacDonald & Company, 1986.

Teegarden, Carol. "Behind These Recipes is a Ghostly Surprise," *Detroit Free Press* (November 26, 1988) 1C, 5C.

Underwood, Peter. *A Host of Hauntings*. London: Leslie Frewin, 1973.

CHAPTER THREE: **Superstition and Folkways**

Black, Algernon. *Without Burnt Offerings*. New York: Viking, 1974.

*Brasch, R. *How Did It Begin?* New York: David McKay, 1965.

*Brown, Raymond Lamont. *A Book of Superstitions*. New York: Taplinger Publishing, 1970.

Clark, Tim. "Straight Facts About Warts (and Some Surefire Cures)." *See* Thomas, pp. 119–121.

Cowan, Lore. *Are You Superstitious?* Princeton, NJ: Apex Books, 1969.

*Garrison, Webb. *How It Started*. Nashville: Abingdon Press, 1972.

Gettings, Fred. *The Book of Palmistry*. London: Triune Books, 1974.

Huxley, Francis. *The Way of the Sacred*. Garden City, NY: Doubleday, 1974.

Jerome, Lawrence. *Astrology Disproved*. Buffalo: Prometheus, 1977.

Opie, Iona, and Peter Opie. *The Lore and Language of Schoolchildren*. Oxford: Oxford University Press, 1959.

*Sifakis, Carl, ed. *Farmer's Almanac 1989*. New York: Country Accents, 1989.

*Smith, Richard Furnald. *Prelude to Science*. New York: Scribners, 1975.

*Thomas, Robert B., ed. *The Old Farmer's Almanac*. Dublin, NH: Yankee Publishing, 1988.

Wills, Gary. "The Tale of a Star Crossed Columnist." United Press Syndicate (June 15, 1988).

CHAPTER FOUR: **Magic and Illusion**

*Blackstone, Harry G. *The Blackstone Book of Magic and Illusion*. New York: Newmarket, 1985.

*Burnham, Tom. *The Dictionary of Misinformation*. New York: Thomas Y. Crowell, 1975.

Charney, David. *Magic: The Great Illusions Revealed and Explained*. Based on *Magic,* by Albert A. Hopkins, first published in 1897. New York: Strawberry Hill, 1975.

Dawes, Edwin A. *The Great Illusionists*. Seacaucus, NJ: Chartwell, 1979.

Fisher, Matthew. "Super Shamaou Flies Across North Battling for Truth, Justice, Inuit Way." *Toronto Globe and Mail* (December 28, 1988) A4.

*Kohn, Alexander. *False Prophets*. Oxford and New York: Basil Blackwell, 1986.

Kohn, Martin. "Moving Magic." *Detroit Free Press* (8 July 1988) B1, B8.

*Lanners, Edi, ed. *Illusions*. New York: Holt, Rinehart, and Winston, 1973.

Randi, James. *Flim Flam*. New York: Lippincott, 1980.

Rawclife, D. H. *Illusions and Delusions of the Supernatural and the Occult*. New York: Dover, 1959. Originally published by Derricke Ridgeway Publishing Co., Ltd., 1952.

*Silverberg, Robert. *A Book of Hoaxes: Scientists and Scoundrels*. New York: Thomas Y. Crowell, 1965.

*Smith, George O. *Scientists' Nightmares*. New York: Putnam's, 1972.

CHAPTER FIVE: Reason and Logic

Bronowski, Jacob. *The Origins of Knowledge*. New Haven, CT: Yale University Press, 1978.

Capaldi, Nicholas. *The Art of Deception*. New York: Scribners, 1971.

Chase, Stuart. *Guides to Straight Thinking*. New York: Harper & Brothers, 1956.

Cohen, Daniel. *Re: Thinking*. New York: Mari Evans, 1982.

* Conan Doyle, Sir Arthur. *Sherlock Holmes: The Complete Novels and Stories*. New York: Bantam, 1986.

*Davidson, Jessica. *The Square Root of Tuesday*. New York: McCall, 1971.

*DeBono, Edward. *Edward DeBono's Thinking Course*. New York: Facts on File, 1985.

Dewey, John. *The Quest for Certainty*. New York: Capricorn, 1929.

Engel, Morris. *With Good Reason*. New York: St. Martin's, 1982.

*Grosswirth, Marvin, and others. *The Mensa Genius Quiz Book*. Reading, MA: Addison-Wesley, 1981.

Hampden-Turner, Charles. *Maps of the Mind*. New York: Collier, 1982.

*Hughes, Patrick, and George Brecht. *Vicious Circles and Infinity*. Garden City, NY: Doubleday, 1975.

Ingle, Dwight. *Is It Really So?* Philadelphia: Westminster, 1976.

*Kohl, Herbert. *A Book of Puzzlements*. New York: Schocken, 1981.

*Morrison, Philip, and Phyllis Morrison. *The Ring of Truth*. New York: Random House, 1984.

*Van Delft, Pieter, and Jack Bottermans. *Creative Puzzles of the World*. New York: H. Abrams, 1978.

CHAPTER SIX: **From Myth to Science**

A Chronological Table of Chinese and World Cultures. Taipei, Taiwan: National Palace Museum, 1985.

Bacon, Francis. *Novum Organum.*

Descartes, René. *Discourse sur la Méthode.*

Gornick, Vivian. *Women in Science.* New York: Simon & Schuster, 1983.

Harman, P. J. *The Scientific Revolution.* London: Methuen, 1983.

Huxley, Francis. *The Way of the Sacred.* Garden City, NY: Doubleday, 1974.

Huxley, Thomas Henry. *Essays upon Some Controverted Questions.* New York: D. Appleton, 1892.

Larsen, Stephen. *The Shaman's Doorway: Opening the Mythic Imagination.* New York: Harper & Row, 1976.

Leeming, David. *Mythology.* New York: Newsweek Books, 1976.

*Meyer, Jerome. *Great Accidents in Science that Changed the World.* New York: Arco, 1967.

Morrison, Philip, and Phyllis Morrison. *The Ring of Truth.* New York: Random House, 1984.

Noddings, Nel, and Paul J. Shore. *Awakening the Inner Eye.* New York: Teachers College Press, 1984.

*Ruchlis, Hy. *Discovering Scientific Method.* New York: Harper & Row, 1963.

*Smith, Richard Furnald. *Prelude to Science.* New York: Scribners, 1975.

Taylor, F. Sherwood. *A Short History of Science.* New York: W. W. Norton, 1949.

*————. *An Illustrated History of Science.* New York: Praeger, 1955.

AFTERWORD: **Future Knowledge**

Campbell, Bob. "Experts Fearful for Man, Nature at African Lake." *Detroit Free Press* (3 May 1989) 3A.

Clarke, Arthur C. *2061: Odyssey Three.* New York: DelRey, 1987.

Conroy, Frank. "Ways We Know and Don't." *Harpers* (November 1988) 63–65.

Crick, Francis. "Lessons from Biology." *Natural History* (November 1988), 67–69. Originally appeared in *What Mad Pursuit?* New York: Basic Books, 1988.

Flanigan, Nancy Ross. "Computer Sees the Light." *Detroit Free Press* (21 April 1989) C1.

————. "Seeing Is Understanding." *Detroit Free Press* (13 December 1988), 1B.

Fromm, Erich. *The Revolution of Hope.* New York: Harper & Row, 1968.

Gassé, Jean-Louis. "This Idiot Savant." *Computerland Magazine* (January/February 1988) 34, 105. Originally appeared in *The Third Apple.* New York: Harcourt Brace Jovanovich, 1987.

Hitching, Francis. *The Mysterious World: An Atlas of the Unexplained.* New York: Holt, Rinehart, 1978.

Hofstadter, Douglas. *Metamagical Themes.* New York: Basic Books, 1985.

Kotulak, Ronald. "Voyage to Venus: A Trip to Earth's Past and Future?" *Chicago Tribune* (2 May 1989).

McLuhan, Marshall. *City as Schoolhouse.* Agincourt, Ontario: Book Society of Canada, Ltd., 1976.

Sudnow, David. *Ways of the Hand.* Cambridge: Harvard University Press, 1978.

Index